LEARNING
AND
TEACHING

By

Dr. D.Sivakumar
Principal
CK College of Education
Jayaram Nagar, Chellankuppam
Cuddalore - 607 002
Tamilnadu (India)

&

Mrs. R. Prabavathi
Assistant Professor of Education
CK College of Education
Cuddalore - 607 002
Tamilnadu (India)

INDIA

Published by:
Namit Wasan
DISCOVERY PUBLISHING HOUSE PVT. LTD.
4383/4B, Ansari Road, Darya Ganj
New Delhi-110 002 (India)
Phone : +91-11-23279245; 23253475; 43596065
E-mail : discoverybooksindia@gmail.com
discoverypublishinghouse@gmail.com
namitwasan9@gmail.com
web : www.discoverypublishinggroup.com

First Edition: **2019**

ISBN: 978-93-88854-16-0

Learning and Teaching

Printed at:
Infinity Imaging Systems
Delhi

Preface

This book entitled "Learning and Teaching" has been written to cover the syllabus of the core paper Learning and Teaching of the B.Ed. Course of Tamil Nadu Teacher Education University, other Universities and Autonomous colleges.

This paper has been included in the B.Ed. Course as per the National Council of Teachers Education's New Regulations after the introduction of B.Ed. Programme for the duration of two years.

This book covered the topics on Nature of learning, Nature of teaching, Behavioral theories of learning, Cognitive and Humanistic theories of learning, Theory of Constructivism, Learner-Centered teaching, Teaching in Diverse classroom, Learning in and out of school, Teacher-Student relationship and finally Teaching as a Profession.

This book will help the B.Ed. students to acquire an indepth Knowledge about all the aspects involved in the teaching learning process. It will give them the general ideas both on different learning process and general approaches to teaching. This would help the Prospective teachers' learn to apply theory and Practical knowledge of teaching learning on specific school contexts, think through and resolve classroom dilemmas more Productively. It would help them understand the various aspects of teaching and create the conditions to ensure effective learning.

This book has been written in a simple, direct and lucid style. The content is precise and specific as the concepts are explained clearly. The content of the topics is interspersed with examples and illustrations. A great effort has been taken to include the current information and the topics. It is hoped that the book will help the readers go a long way in becoming excellent teachers as we believe, as do many, that learning and teaching are correlated, and that in many cases a good teacher makes a good learner.

–Authors

Contents

1

Nature of Learning

INTRODUCTION

Learning is one of the most important mental functions of humans, animals and artificial cognitive systems. It relies on the acquisition of different types of knowledge supported by perceived information. It leads to the development of new capacities, skills, values, understanding, and preferences. Its goal is the increasing of individual and group experience. Learning functions can be performed by different brain learning processes, which depend on the mental capacities of learning subject, the type of knowledge which has to be acquitted, as well as on socio-cognitive and environmental circumstances. Learning ranges from simple forms of learning such as habituation and classical conditioning seen in many animal species, to more complex activities such as play, seen only in relatively intelligent animals and humans. Therefore, in general, learning can be either a conscious or non-conscious process.

For example, in small children, non-conscious learning processes are as natural as breathing. In fact, there is evidence for behavioral learning prenatally, in which habituation has been observed as early as 32 weeks into gestation, indicating that the central nervous system is sufficiently developed and primed for learning and memory to occur very early on in development.

MEANING

From the educational point of view, the process of modification of behavior is termed as learning. From the psychological point of view, learning implies making the most appropriate response to stimulus. Learning is the acquisition of habits, knowledge and attitudes. It involves new ways of doing things and it operates in an individual's attempts to overcome obstacles or to adjust to new situations. When learning takes place, it can be expected that a more or less permanent change will be evidenced in the learner's behavior.

DEFINITIONS

- "Learning is not acquiring knowledge or skill by mere mechanical repetitions" - *Skinner*
- "Learning is the process by which an organism in satisfying its motivation adopts and adjusts its behavior in order to overcome abstracts or barriers" - *Kingly & Gray*
- "Learning is shown by a change in behavior as a result of experiences" - *Cronback*
- "Learning is change in behavior resulting from others" - *J.P.Guilford*
- "Learning is a modification of both behavior and the way of perceiving" - *Murphy*
- "Learning is the name given to a small number of demonstrable relationship between environmental factors (Stimuli) and behavioral changes" - *E.C.Tolman*

NATURE OF LEARNING

1. Learning is adaption

Learning occupies a very important place in our life. Learning is the process of change which enables an organism to adjust itself to the environment, it is therefore a process of development and growth, and it is characterized by flexibility because the individual has to adapt itself constantly to the circumstances of the environment.

2. Learning is active

Learning does not take place without a purpose and self activity. In teaching learning process, the activity learner counts more than the activity of the teacher.

3. Learning brings behavioral changes

Learning brings the progressive changes in the behavioral of an individual

4. Learning is improvement

Learning is often considered as a process of improvement with practice or training. We learn many things which help us to improve our performance.

5. Learning is organizing experience

Learning occurs both in formal and informal situations. New choice, new beliefs and new interest are aroused in them and this learning process termed as formal learning. Apart from these he/she learns informally from their other experiences. So learning is not mere addition of knowledge. It is the reorganization of experience.

6. Learning is goal directed

It purpose or goal, which determines what the learner sees in the learning situations and how he acts. If there is no purpose or goal, learning can be hardly seen.

7. Learning is problem solving

Learning involves problem solving, it helps to understand and discover relations between different contents in situation. Learning is an automatic process. It takes place when the child becomes active. He/She have to include him/her in the process of learning.

8. Learning is Universal and Continuous

All living creatures learn. Every moment the individual engages himself to learn more and more. Right from the birth till death the learning continues.

9. Learning is unenforceable

Human learning is a matter of human action; it cannot be enforced upon the human beings. Most pupils are, generally, able to comply with normal expectations. But when any child is not, the teacher must wait for that child to be ready for learning or he will destroy the very work which is being attempted. It is a characteristic of learning that it is unenforceable.

10. Learning is a product of the environment

Learning cannot take place in vacuum-it can only take place in relation to environment. The environment should be healthy and rich in educative possibilities. It must be conductive to learning.

IMPORTANCE OF LEARNING

- Learning plays a central role in the language we speak our customs, attitudes, beliefs, our goals and our personality traits.
- Learning creates motivation to learn or gain something.
- It develops our knowledge.
- It creates our curiosity to know something.
- It creates the ability to the sense of discrimination, ability to use symbols.
- Learning provides the skill of creativity.
- Learning helps to solve any problem in one's life.
- Learning provides experiences in our life.
- Learning modulates our attitude and aptitude.

CHARACTERISTICS OF LEARNING

W.R. McCaw in his book "Educational Psychology" has given the detail of the characteristics of learning process. They are:

- Learning is a continuous change in behavior. It is a lifelong process.
- It is comprehensive. It affects every aspects of human life.
- Learning is physically, mentally and cognitively attached with the whole of the person.
- Learning brings changes in the discipline of behavior.

- Learning is developmental.
- Learning is encouragement. Sometimes it becomes more influential motivator than some direct stimulus such as fear of punishment.
- Learning is always directed towards a goal, and all the behavior of the learner are modified in such a way that he/she may reach that goal.
- Learning and interest are linked with each other. An individual learns better than he/she becomes interested in their particular subject.
- Learning depends upon motivation and readiness.

ELEMENTS OF LEARNING

The four basic elements of learning are:

(i) **Motivation:** In learning the motivation is something that energizes, directs, and sustains behavior; it gets students moving, points them in a particular direction, and keeps them going.

(ii) **Reinforcement:** The reinforcement encourages or establishing a belief in their learning process. It makes strengthening the student's learning.

(iii) **Retention:** The student has to remember what they have learnt. Achieves are done through the retention.

(iv) **Transference:** Transference is the ability to extend what has been learnt in one context to other contexts. It is an important learning outcome for education. Factual knowledge and understanding are necessary pre-requisites for transference.

Other Elements of Learning are:

1. **Face-to-face promotive interaction** - refers to students talking to each other in order to share insights and ideas.
2. **Individual responsibility** - refers to holding students accountable for themselves to prevent "freeloading" in a learning group.
3. **Collaborative skills** - include skills necessary for effective group functioning, such as leadership, teambuilding, and conflict resolution.

4. **Group processing** - refers to how well the group is functioning aside from the academic products or performances.
5. **Positive interdependence** - the perception among members of the group that "we sink or swim together."
6. **Ability:** The students' native ability dictates the prospects of success in any purposeful activity. It determines their capacity to understand and assimilate information for their own use and application.
7. **Aptitude:** It refers to the students' innate talent or gift. It indicates a natural capacity to learn certain skills.
8. **Interests:** Learners vary in activities that are undertaken due to a strong appeal or attraction. Lessons that give the learners the chance to express themselves will be more meaningful and easily absorbed
9. **Family and Cultural background:** Students who come from different socio economic background manifest a wide range of behavior due to difference in upbringing practices.
10. **Attitudes:** Attitude refers to an individual perspective and disposition. Some positive attitudes are curiosity, responsibility, creativity & persistence.
11. **The learner or the pupil is involved:** Unless the pupil is prepared or enabled to learn, learning cannot take place. Learning is a very personal experience. We cannot "give" this experience to a child.
12. **The Experience:** "The experience or the situation provides that experience which causes learning". These situations are provided by the school in the form of subjects, activities or atmosphere and the teacher organizes them for the pupils.
13. **The teacher is the key person:** In the learning process, the teacher is the key person. He is to organize learning experiences for children and the child would learn by reacting to such experiences. The teacher cannot make a child learn. He can only facilitate the learning process

by properly organizing experiences and creating a conductive climate for learning, e.g., arranging facilities, providing materials and gadgets, managing social relationships and activities which promise rich, worthwhile productive living for children.

14. **The climate:** The climate or the environment is an important element in learning in school. It can stimulate or retard learning.

In an effective learning situation, these five elements should satisfy the following conditions.

(a) Instructor – He/She should:

- Have clear objectivc.
- Know the subject matter and have it well organized.
- Be able to communicate with learner.
- Allow learners participation, ask for it.
- Use a definite teaching plan.
- Speak loudly and clearly so that all can hear and understand.
- Be skillful in use of teaching materials and equipments.

(b) Learner should:

- Have need for information.
- Be interested.
- Be capable of learning.
- Use the information again.

(c) Subject Matter should be:

- Related to learners need.
- Applicable to real situation.
- Thought intellectual levels of the learners.
- Well organized and logically and clearly presented.
- Challenging and satisfying.
- Fulfilling overall objectives.

(d) Physical Facilities

- Free from outside destruction.
- The room should be well lighted.
- Adequate space for the group.

(e) Teaching Equipments

- Meet the needs effectively.
- Readily available.
- In working order.

PRINCIPLES OF LEARNING

(i) **Readiness:** Readiness implies a degree of concentration and eagerness. Individuals learn best when they are physically, mentally and emotionally ready to learn, and do not learn well it they see no reason for learning. Getting students ready to learn, creating interest by showing the value of the subject matter, and providing continuous mental or physical challenge, is usually the instructors' responsibility.

(ii) **Exercise:** The principle of exercise states that those things most often repeated are best remembered. It is the basis of drill and practice. It has been proven that students learn best and retain information longer when they have meaningful practice and repetition.

(iii) **Effect:** The principle of effect is based on the emotional reaction of the student. It has a direct relationship to motivation. The principle of effect is that learning is strengthened when accompanied by a pleasant or satisfying feeling, and the learning is weakened when associated with an unpleasant feeling, every learning experience should contain elements that leave the student with some good feelings.

(iv) **Primacy:** The state of being first often creates a strong, almost unshakable, impression. Things learned first create a strong impression in the mind that is difficult to erase. This means that what is taught must be right the first time. The student's first experience should be

positive, functional, and lay the foundation for all that is to follow. What the student learns must be procedurally correct and applied the very first time.

(v) **Regency:** The principle of regency states that things most recently learners are best remembered. Conversely, the further a student is removed time-wise from a new fact or understanding, the more difficult it is to remember. For example it is fairly easy to recall a telephone number dialed a few minutes ago, but it is usually impossible to recall a new number dialed last week.

(vi) **Intensity:** The principle of intensity implies that a student will learn more from the real thing than from a substitute. For example, a student can get more understanding and appreciation of a movie by watching it than by reading the script. Likewise, a student is likely to gain greater understanding of tasks by performing them rather than merely reading about them.

(vii) **Requirement:** The law of requirement states that "We must have something to obtain or do something". It can be ability, skill, instrument or anything that may help us to learn or gain something.

(viii) **Freedom:** The principle of freedom states that things freely are best learned. Conversely, the further a student is coerced, the more difficult is for him to learn, assimilate and implement what is learned. Since learning is an active process, students must have freedom: freedom of choice, freedom of action, freedom to bear the results of action – these are the three great freedoms that constitute personal responsibility. If no freedom is granted, students may have little interest in learning.

Implications for Teaching Process in Learning

(i) ***Learning is a process of active construction:*** Learning is the interaction between what students know, the new information they encounter, and the activities they engage in as they learn.

Teaching Implications: Provide opportunities for students to connect with the content in a variety of meaningful ways by using cooperative learning, interactive lectures, engaging assignments, hands-on lab/ field experiences, and other active learning strategies.

(ii) ***Students' prior knowledge is an important determinant of what they will learn:*** Students do not come to the class as a blank slate. They use what they already know about a topic to interpret new information. When students cannot relate new material to what they already know, they tend to memorize—learning for the test—rather than developing any real understanding of the content.

Teaching Implications: Learn about the students' experiences, preconceptions, or misconceptions by using pre-tests, background knowledge probes, and written or oral activities designed to reveal students' thinking about the topic.

(iii) ***Organizing information into a conceptual framework helps students remember and use knowledge:*** Students must learn factual information, understand these facts and ideas in the context of a conceptual framework, and organize knowledge in ways that facilitate retrieval and application in order to develop competence in a new topic.

Teaching Implications: Support students by using concept maps, flowcharts, outlines, comparison tables, etc., to make the structure of the knowledge clear.

(iv) ***Learning is a social phenomenon:*** Students learn with greater understanding when they share ideas through conversation, debate, and negotiation. Explaining a concept to one's peers puts knowledge to a public test where it can be examined, reshaped, and clarified.

Teaching Implications: Use Cooperative learning strategies, long-term group projects, class discussions, and group activities to support the social side of learning.

(v) ***Learning is context-specific:*** It is often difficult for students to use what they learn in class in new contexts (i.e., other classes, the workplace, or their personal lives).

Teaching Implications: Use problem-based learning, simulations or cases, and service learning to create learning environments similar to the real world.

ROTE LEARNING

Rote learning is a learning technique which focuses on memorization. The major practice involved in rote learning is learning by repetition by which pupils commit information to memory in a highly structured way. This is as opposed to critical thinking or problem solving, in which students are forced to apply the concepts they have learned to theoretical or example problems.

In rote learning the students are able to quickly recall these basic facts when asked. The downside is that with a lack of critical thinking application, students may have trouble applying the facts they have learned to real-world situations. The main disadvantage of rote learning is that it is boring and extremely limited.

The two biggest examples of rote learning are the alphabet and numbers.

MEANINGFUL LEARNING

Meaningful learning refers to the concept that the learned knowledge is fully understood by the individual and that the individual knows how that specific fact relates to other stored facts.

Advantages:

- Focuses on the product or outcome of the learning process.
- Focuses on understanding information not memorization.
- Encourage active learning techniques such as cooperative learning, problem-based learning, case-based learning and team based learning.

Disadvantages:

- Must build on previously learned knowledge.
- Limited capacity of working memory causes a struggle.

- Students who lack prior knowledge get very little out of active learning sessions.
- Can only be utilized when students have a knowledge base relatable to new material.

Differences between Rote Learning and Meaningful Learning

S.No.	Rote Learning	Meaningful Learning
1.	Verbatim memorization of new information.	Concept is fully understood by individual.
2.	No connection between new and previous knowledge.	New information is related to what students already know (Prior Knowledge).
3.	It cannot be utilize in their practical life.	It can be utilize in their practical life.
4.	Students are considered as empty vessels to be filled with the lecture of a teacher.	It develops students' skills and improving their attitudes/values.
5.	Achieves only retention of new information.	Achieves both retention and transfer, and even achieves retention better than rote learning.
6.	Present definitions, formulas, and new information without explaining relationship with students' experiences.	Relate information to everyday experiences.

ACTIVE LEARNING

Active learning is generally defined as any instructional method that engages students in the learning process. In short, active learning requires students to do meaningful learning activities and think about what they are doing.

ELEMENTS OF ACTIVE LEARNING

The four important basic elements of active learning is:

- Talking and Listening
- Writing
- Reading
- Reflecting

NATURE OF ACTIVE LEARNING

Active learning is about learning by doing. It is especially common in:

- Laboratory, practical and studio classes
- Discussions in class and on-line
- Fieldwork
- Learning in and from work-based activities
- Problem-based and inquiry-based learning
- Independent learning
- Peer teaching
- Role playing and simulations

Techniques

- **Class discussion:** It may be held in person or in an online environment. It is best that these discussions be centered on an open-ended (occasionally controversial) topic (eg. one that has no right or wrong answer).
- **Small group discussion:** It is a similar activity between individual, groups, or teams of individuals. A presidential debate is a common debate format. But these also may center around controversial or political topic.
- **Think-pair-share activity:** It is when learners take a minute to ponder the previous lesson, later to discuss it with one or more of their peers, finally to share it with the class a part of a formal discussion.
- **Short written exercise:** It is often used is the "one minute paper." In this exercise students are asked to summarize the day's discussion in a short paper to be turned in before the end of class. This is a good way to review materials.
- **Peer Review:** Students review and comment on materials written by their classmates.
- **Game based learning:** Uses competitive exercises, either pitting the students against each other or through computer simulations.

PRINCIPLES OF ACTIVE LEARNING

The suggested principles of active learning are:

- **Purposive:** the relevance of the task with the students' concerns.
- **Reflective:** students' reflection on the meaning of what is learnt.
- **Negotiated:** negotiation of goals and methods of learning between students and teachers.
- **Critical:** students appreciate different ways and means of learning the content.
- **Complex:** students compare learning tasks with complexities existing in real life and making reflective analysis.
- **Situation-driven:** the need of the situation is considered in order to establish learning tasks.
- **Engaged:** real life tasks are reflected in the activities conducted for learning.

STRATEGIES OF ACTIVE LEARNING

Active learning can be achieved through a variety of instructional strategies. Decisions about which strategy to use will consider several dimensions:

- the amount of class time required
- the degree of structure and planning
- the pattern of interaction (i.e. between faculty and students or among students)
- students' prior knowledge of the subject matter

IMPORTANCE OF ACTIVE LEARNING

The active learning imposes:

- Increased content knowledge, critical thinking and problem-solving abilities, and positive attitudes towards learning in comparison to traditional lecture-based delivery.
- Increased enthusiasm for learning in both students and instructors.

- Development of graduate capabilities such as critical and creative thinking, problem-solving, adaptability, communication and interpersonal skills.
- Improving students' perceptions and attitudes towards information literacy.

SELF LEARNING

Self-Learning is an individualized method of learning. Self-learning imposes where the learner is free to chose what to learn, how to learn, when to learn and where to learn.

Four Tiers of Self Learning

(i) **Learning by Preparing:** Exploring interest, extending knowledge, creating ideas, envisioning possibilities.

(ii) **Learning by Doing:** Conducting activities, developing skills, overcoming obstacles, achieving goals.

(iii) **Learning by Reflecting on Doing:** Recording project history, analyzing the process employed, reflected on personal performance, assessing success.

(iv) **Learning by Moving Forward:** Celebrating success, considering "Where am I now?", Imagine possible futures, etc.

IMPORTANCE OF SELF LEARNING

Self learning possess the individual to:

- Become an independent thinker.
- Learn to accept responsibility.
- Gain the freedom to learn without restrictions and earns accountability.
- Give the opportunity to develop a good work ethic.

CONCLUSION

Learning occupies very important role in our life. Everyone has understanding, resources, and interests on which to build. Learning a topic does not begin from knowing nothing to learning that is based on entirely new information. Many kinds of learning require transforming existing understanding, especially when one's understanding needs to be applied in new situations. Teachers have a critical role in assisting learners to engage their understanding, building on learners' understandings, correcting misconceptions, and observing and engaging with learners during the processes of learning. In this Unit, meaning of learning, its definition, elements of learning, basic principles of learning and their implications, rote learning, meaningful learning, active learning and self-learning were discussed in detail.

QUESTIONS

1. Give the meaning and definitions of learning.
2. Describe the elements of learning.
3. What are the basic principles of learning?
4. Discuss about the rote learning and meaningful learning.
5. How would you implicate the active learning?
6. Write an essay on self- learning.

2

Nature of Teaching

INTRODUCTION

Teaching is a simple term, it referred as a either an occupation or profession of a group of peoples known as teacher or an activity or activities to help an individual to learn or acquire some knowledge, skills, attitudes or interests. Teaching is a form of interpersonal influence aimed to change the behavior potential of another person. B.O. Smith (1960). Teaching is a system of actions intends to produce learning. Above all a good or effective teaching must accomplished the following objectives: (1) It should tell whether teaching is a process or product. (2) It should clearly indicate its constitutional elements or factors. (3) It should reveal its objectives. (4) It should say about its organizational or structural aspects. Thus, "Teaching is a triadic relation and tripolar process involving the source of teaching, student and a set of activities and manipulation to bring changes in the behavior of the students".

MEANING

Teaching is a noble profession. The act or business of instructing; also, that which is taught; instruction. Teaching is the knowledge taught to students, learners. Teaching is the one injecting knowledge, lessons, methods etc., The Teaching for Understanding framework is a guide that can help keep the focus of educational practice on developing student understanding. Teaching a particular subject, a particular lesson or lessons to the students is called teaching.

Teaching is important for endless reasons. Although I've been in the classroom for only a few short weeks I realize that I have taught my whole life each and every day, just different things in different ways. I have also come to realize that being a teacher means that I have a lot to learn myself. In fact, I have never needed to learn more than I do now, even though ironically I am now the one teaching. Each day, each class, every student with whom I interact, I have the unique opportunity to touch their life. In the couple weeks I've spent in the classroom I can already see the transformational nature of this career. But ultimately, teaching is important because teaching is our future.

DEFINITIONS

- "Teaching is a form of interpersonal influence aimed at changing the behavior potential of another person."

  - Gage
- "Teaching is an interactive process, primarily involving class room talk which takes place between teacher and pupil and occurs during certain definable activity."

  - Edmund Amidon
- "Teaching is the arrangement of contingencies of reinforcement." *- Skinner*

TYPES OF TEACHING

There are two type of teaching :

- Formal-Which is systemic deliberate direct and consciously impart by specially
- Informal-it is teaching one get the outside of class room

What is effective teaching?

Effective teaching is the teaching that successfully achieves the learning objectives by the pupils as identified by the teacher. The most effective teaching is that which results in the most effective learning. In addition, the learning is a process not the product, it involves all those experiences and training through teaching of an individual, which helps to change the behavior and prepare to take necessary adjustment and adaptation in change situation. The root of effective teaching of a successful teacher is evolved in the following tenets: (1) Pupils learn best in a positive and nurturing environment established by teachers who believe that every pupil is capable of learning. (2) All pupils have areas of strengths and interests that can be useful in advancing pupil learning. Effective teachers establish an instructional environment that will draw on these strengths. (3) Teachers take into account the whole pupil; in other words, they attend to the cognitive, affective, social, and physical dimensions when developing an instructional program. (4) Active engagement and interaction facilitate pupil learning. (5) New learning is built upon previously learned information. Learning is enhanced when prior knowledge and cultural and social experiences are valued, acknowledged, and leveraged throughout the curriculum. (6) Pupil learning is both individually and socially constructed; it is influenced by cultural, familial, and social context. (7) Meaningful assessment is both formative and summative; it relies on multiple measures, including informal observations.

CHARACTERISTICS OF GOOD TEACHING

(i) **Demonstrates Classroom Management Skills:** Teacher has an organized approach to classroom learning, effective classroom management skills, and is able to pace the curriculum. Teacher sets appropriate behavioral standards and enforces them consistently.

(ii) **Engages Students in Learning:** Teacher motivates students to be continually engaged in learning activities. Teacher has knowledge of child development and corresponding age characteristics and needs. Teacher is responsive to individual student learning styles, knowledgeable about varied instructional strategies and materials, and makes appropriate decisions about how to use them. Teacher relates the curriculum to the appropriate learning context. Teacher strives to meet the needs and abilities of the classroom student population.

(iii) **Encourages Parent Involvement:** Teacher is sensitive to and respects the diversity of parents; native language and cultures. Teacher is pro-active in reaching out to communicate with parents and involve them in classroom and school wide activities as well as other forms of parent involvement. Teacher has awareness of and sensitivity to students' family circumstances.

(iv) **Fosters Professional Collegiality:** Teacher respects other teacher's styles of teaching and has a friendly approach to working with school staff and community, sharing effective practices, engaging in problem-solving and similar activities.

(v) **Maintains an ongoing commitment to learning:** Teacher says current with educational research and trends in subject areas. Teacher is open to learning new approaches and techniques and shares information with pupils. Teacher has enthusiasm for learning and able to reflect and grow as a professional. Teacher makes use of community and other outside resources both for student growth and own professional growth.

(vi) **Possesses Knowledge of subject matter:** Teacher has command of subject matter and uses appropriate instructional materials. Teacher is able to present information in a clear and effective manner.

(vii) **Promotes Positive Learning Outcomes:** Teacher has high expectations for all students. Teacher recognizes and develops instructional strategies appropriate for individual student learning styles, language proficiency, cultural background, and disabling conditions. Teacher regularly assesses student learning and adjusts instruction according to evidence of student growth. Teacher strives to realize educational goals set of students.

(viii) **Supports an atmosphere of mutual respect:** Teacher sets a good example for students: punctual, courteous, concerned about others, and so on. Teacher respects each student as an individual and encourages mutual respect in the classroom. Teacher listens and pays attention to

what students are saying; respects individual learning styles as well as cultural diversity, language differences, and disabling conditions.

COMMON CHARACTERISTICS OF GOOD TEACHING

According to UNESCO (2004), the main characteristics of good teaching relate to a number of broad categories:

- ***Relevance:*** of the teaching content, in particular alignment with the curriculum.
- ***Sufficient learning time:*** this refers to the time devoted to actual teaching, as opposed to the official hours set in the curriculum.
- Structured teaching, in which learners' engagement is stimulated, their understanding monitored, and feedback and reinforcement regularly provided.
- A conducive classroom environment with, in particular, a task-oriented climate, mutual respect between the students and teacher and among students themselves, orderliness, and safety.
- Teachers with appropriate subject matter mastery, verbal intelligence, a broad teaching repertoire, and motivation to achieve.

VIEW OF GREAT THINKERS AND PHILOSOPHERS ON TEACHING

(i) **Aristotle:** Aristotle suggested the inductive and deductive methods of teaching. He was the first to formulate the logic of these procedures. He applied these methods both for the objective and subjective studies. It is in the respect that he is considered as the father of modern sciences.

(ii) **Plato:** According to him the 3Rs (reading, writing and counting) are very important in Education. Plato recommended play method at elementary level. Student should learn by doing. Plato believes imitation to be of the greatest importance, for he realizes that the child learns a great deal through imitation. He was against the use of force in education. Plato gave importance to

nursery education, as nursery education plays a vital role in the education of man and it helps to build his/her moral character and state of mind.

Plato stressed that the teacher should be:

- The teacher is like torch bearer who leads a man lying in the dark cave, out of the darkness into the bright light of the outside world.
- The teacher is thus the constant guide of the students.
- The teacher must be a person of high integrity and must possess high self worth.
- He/She must have pleasing personality, in depth knowledge and professional training.
- Teachers should lead a true moral life. They should practice what they preach.

(iii) **Gandhiji:** He stressed the learning by doing, activity method, and questioning/discussion method. According to him, the medium of instruction is followed by the mother tongue. He expected that the teachers would make attractive and intelligible. Based on his view, the teacher should be:

- Dedication
- Ready to serve the masses
- Well Trained
- Proficient
- Men of Knowledge
- Enthusiasm
- Faith and commitment in teaching

(iv) **Montessori:** She encourages teachers to view children and classroom education differently than the common teacher-student relationship. Instead of focusing on academic education, he tended to focus on respecting and encouraging each child's individual differences, providing a nurturing environment to teach social interaction and emotional skills.

The teacher acts as a guide, watching over the classroom to remove obstacles from learning but not participating as a direct instructor. Instead of instructing with rote lectures, handouts, worksheets, and lesson plans, a Montessori teacher will offer guidance, but the child is ultimately responsible for his or her own individual learning.

(v) **John Amos Comenius:** Among the following statements of Comenius may be found some of the traditional maxims of teaching method.

- **Easy to difficult:** Proceed from what is easy to what is more difficult.
- **General to Particular:** Instead of the maxim 'Proceed from the particular to the general' we find 'proceed from general to the particular'.
- **The inductive method of teaching:** This is expressed thus: It is necessary that examples come before rules.

(vi) **John Dewey**

Pragmatic education grants considerable importance to the educator, who is conceived as a servant of society. His task is to create in the school an environment which will help in the development of the child's social personality and enable the child's to become a responsible democratic citizen. Dewey considers the educator to be so important that he goes so far as to call him God's representative on earth.

In order to realize the values of equality and independence in the school, the teacher should not treat himself as superior to the children. He/She must also consciously from imposing his/her own ideas, interest, views and tendencies on children. Hence, it is essential for the educator to pay constant attention to the individual differences to the children.

(vii) **Sir Aurobindo:** He possessed the following three principles of teaching:

- The first principle is that nothing can be taught.

- The Second principle is that the mind should be constantly consulted in its growth.
- The third principle is to work from the near to the far from that which is to that which shall be.

REFLECTIVE TEACHING

Recently, the concept of reflection has been widely used in a variety of different teacher education programs in order to help pre- and in-service teachers in the process of clarifying their ideas about their own teaching practices, and in considering and evaluating those ideas in the hope that they will develop the capacity to evaluate and improve their teaching practices. Therefore, reflection has become the part of teacher education programs, and such terms as 'reflective teaching', 'reflective practice', 'reflective thinking', 'the teacher as decision-maker' 'the teacher as researcher' and 'the teacher as reflective practitioner' are now widely used in a variety of educational contexts and are informed by diverse theoretical frameworks.

MEANING

Reflective teaching is a personal tool that teachers can use to observe and evaluate the way they behave in their classroom. It can be both a private process as well as one that you discuss with colleagues. When you collect information regarding what went on in your classroom and takes the time to analyze it from a distance, you can identify more than just what worked and what didn't. You will be able to look at the underlying principles and beliefs that define the way that you work. This kind of self-awareness is a powerful ally for a teacher, especially when so much of what and how they teach can change in the moment.

DEFINITION

According to Jack Richards, reflection or "critical reflection, refers to an activity or process in which an experience is recalled, considered, and evaluated, usually in relation to a broader purpose. It is a response to past experience and involves conscious recall and examination of the experience as a basis for evaluation and decision-making and as a source for planning and action. (Richard 1990)

According to Bartlett, reflective teacher involves moving beyond a primary concern with instructional techniques and "how to" questions and asking "what" and "why" questions that regard instructions and managerial techniques not as ends in themselves, but as part of broader educational purposes. Asking "what and why" questions give us a certain power over our teaching. We could claim that the degree of autonomy and responsibility we have in our work as teachers is determined by the level of control we can exercise over our actions. In reflecting on the above kind of questions, we begin to exercise control and open up the possibility of transforming our everyday classroom life. (Bartlett, 1990)

BECOMING A REFLECTIVE TEACHER AND HIS CHARACTERISTICS

It has been said by many teacher that for learning to occur, the learner must be taken out of his or her comfort zone. The idea behind this is that to truly learn something significant, there needs to be an element of struggle. It is a fine line because students should not be struggling to the point where they get too frustrated or give up, but they need to realize that they do not know it or cannot do it already. They need to understand what they do not know, what they need to know, and why they need to know it to move forward with mastering a new skill or content. Otherwise, why are they wasting their time learning something that they already know or that will not help them? This idea should not be applied to students but to learners; as educators, we need to be continually learning and improving. I posit that to improve in any meaningful way, educators need to be reflective. They need to be constantly discerning what they know, what their strengths and weaknesses are, and what they need to do to improve. Just as importantly, they need to be thinking along these lines not just about themselves, but about all of their students.

- Examines his or her own reactions to children or their actions to understand their source.

- Is curious about children's play and watchers it closely
- Changes the environment and materials to encourage new play and learning possibilities.
- The reflective teacher has time set aside specifically for thinking about his professional practice, growth needs, and students' needs.
- The reflective teacher takes action upon his focused thoughts about professional practice. He does not continue in a course of action that he has realized is not working.
- The reflective teacher analyzes his own lessons to see what worked and what did not. He makes changes as necessary. When a lesson does not go well, which will happen to everyone, he learns from it and does not teach the lesson the same way again.
- The reflective teacher recognizes the inherent differences in his classes (when he has more than one group of students) and does not treat all classes the same by teaching exactly the same lesson.
- The reflective teacher takes planned time within class to determine the efficacy of the lesson and take steps to improve it, if need be.
- The reflective teacher knows both his strengths and his students' strengths. His lessons are designed around their strengths and areas of interest to maximize learning.
- The reflective teacher is cognizant of his own weaknesses and takes planned steps to improve in those areas.
- The reflective teacher seeks feedback from many sources, such as other teachers, students, parents, and administrators. He is open to constructive criticism.
- The reflective teacher understands that he cannot optimally teach students by himself. Teaching is a complex field and it takes help from many others.
- The reflective teacher shares his experience with the understanding that it can benefit others who may be able to learn from his experiences.

MY GOALS AS A TEACHER

A teacher is not what I have always wanted to be. As a matter of fact, it wasn't until I had taken several of my general studies classes that I made a commitment to teach. Having played football through middle school and high school, I just assumed that whatever I did would have to be related to football. It was, however, during a time of reflection that I thought about a former football coach and the rapport that he had with me and other players. He wanted to bring out the best in each of us. It was then that I realized that I wanted to do the same.

An architect can hope to design affordable homes for people in need but may not necessarily meet every person who benefits from his noble intentions. But teachers have direct interactions with the people they're helping, and whatever their goals may be, this allows them to see these goals realized.

Goals for teaching are highly individualized. They're not in it for the time off or the recognition they're in it to make a difference, to learn and to inspire, and they teach because they realize the value of education. Only you can set goals for yourself. Only you know why you want to teach. But no matter what those specific goals are, they can pretty much be summed into a single goal: You want to help people. And there are many ways you can help someone as a teacher. To name a few, teachers aspire to educate, to inspire, to learn and to affect positive change.

1. Educate

A great teacher should love educating students, and one of the principal goals many teachers set for themselves is to be the best educator they can be. There is something extremely gratifying about imparting information to your students and working with them to ensure they understand not only concepts, but practical applications as well. There are different methods you can use to teach, and while your teaching style is unique to you, the most important thing is that you engage, motivate and inspire students to learn. Many people teach out of a passion for their subject. If you truly love a particular topic, you may have a desire to share that knowledge with others indeed that passion can make you excel at it.

2. Inspire

Teachers seek to inspire students in all aspects of their lives, and for many teachers, their greatest goal is to be a role model. A role model is someone who inspires and encourages students to strive for greatness, and teaches them through experience and commitment how to realize their full potential to become the best they can be. Teachers can inspire an uninterested student to become engrossed in learning. They can motivate them to participate and focus, and even bring introverted students out of their shells. A great teacher can get students reading, inspire a passion for languages, and make math or science fun, and turn history lessons into fun and exciting stories.

3. Learn

Teaching is one of those careers where you learn something new every day, and many educators cite this as one of the main things they hope to get out of their career. On a strictly professional level, the education you attain to become a teacher opens your eyes to many things you may never have been exposed to before. Teachers also learn a great deal about themselves through teaching.

4. Change

Ambitious teachers are the ones who enter this career to affect change. These are the ones who want to meet the demand for great teachers: They make it their goal to help improve the quality of education for everyone.

CONCLUSION

In its broadest sense, teaching is a process that facilitates learning. Teaching is the specialized application of knowledge, skills and attributes designed to provide unique service to meet the educational needs of the individual and of society. The choice of learning activities whereby the goals of education are realized in the school is the responsibility of the teaching profession. In addition to providing students with learning opportunities to meet curriculum outcomes, teaching emphasizes the development of values and guides students in their social relationships. Teachers employ practices that develop positive self-concept in students. As teaching takes place in a classroom setting, the direct interaction between teacher and student is the most important element in teaching. From the above said, we come to know that teaching plays a vital role in developing knowledge and behavioral changes in the learners for their future.

QUESTIONS

1. Give the meaning and definitions of teaching.
2. List out the characteristics of good teaching.
3. Mention the views of great thinkers and philosophers on teaching.
4. Write an essay on - becoming a reflective teacher.
5. "My goals as a teacher"- Discuss.

3

Behavioural Theories of Learning

INTRODUCTION

Learning is an adaptive function by which our nervous system changes in relation to stimuli in the environment, thus changing our behavioural responses and permitting us to function in our environment. The process occurs initially in our nervous system in response to environmental stimuli. Neural pathways can be strengthened, pruned, activated, or rerouted, all of which cause changes in our behavioral responses.

Every learning theory serves two purposes. One is that it gives detailed information about human behavior, supplies material for further research, brings to surface some new facts and above all guides man in his search of ultimate truth. Secondly, a theory explains the relationship between different factors and interaction among them and its outcome.

BEHAVIOURIST APPROACH TO LEARNING

According to behaviourism, learning is a mechanical process of associating the stimulus with response, which produces a new behavior. Such behavior is strengthened by the reinforcement. Behaviourists view the learner as a passive Person, who responds to the stimuli.

According to them, the learner starts as 'tabula rasa' (which means clean slate) and the behavior is shaped by reinforcement. Positive as well as negative reinforcement increase the probability of the repetition of behavior.

However, the punishment decreases the chance of repetition of the behaviour. Learning is therefore defined as a change in the behavior of the learner.

The behaviourist school sees the mind as a "Black box" in the sense that a response to a stimulus can be observed quantitatively, totally ignoring the effect of thought processes occurring in the mind. The school, therefore, looks at overt behaviours that can be observed and measured as indicators of learning.

KEY IDEAS OF BEHAVIOURISM

The key ideas of behaviourism are as follows:

- Behaviourism focuses on observable learning events as demonstrated by stimulus and response relationship.
- Learning always involves a change in behavior.
- Mental processes should be excluded from the scientific study of learning.
- The laws governing learning apply equally to all organisms, including human organisms.
- Organisms begin life as blank slates there are no innate laws of behavior.
- Learning result from external events in the environment.
- Behaviourism is a deterministic theory: the subject has no choice but to responds to appropriate stimuli.

Behaviourist Aassumption about Learning

The main assumption of behaviourist learning is as follow:

- Observable behavior is more important than understanding internal activities;
- Behaviour should be focused on simple element: specific stimuli and responses;
- Learning is about behavior change.

KEY PRINCIPLES OF BEHAVIOURISM

The key principles of behaviorisms are as follows:

- **Reinforcement:** positive or negative feedback which will lead the learner to from a strong association between the stimulus and the desired behavior.

- **Contiguity:** the more immediate the feedback, the stronger the association.
- **Repetition:** The more frequent the stimulus generalizes the response.
- **Variation:** Varying the pattern of the stimulus generalizes the response.
- **Intermittent Reinforcement:** Not reward; it helps keep the learner guessing.
- **Extinction:** If the stimulus-response bond is not reinforced the association will die.

BEHAVIOURAL APPROACHES TO LEARNING

Common behavoiural approaches to learning are as follows:

- The learner takes on a predominantly passive and reactive role.
- Instruction is structured and systematic.
- Concrete and defined instructional goals, objectives and strategies aimed at learner in general and not on the individual learner.
- Learning can be measured.
- It assumes that a well-planned instructional intervention can result in a desired learning outcome.
- Focus on Simplification (start with easy and progress to more difficult) and repetition (rote learning/drill and practice).
- Instruction is instructor-Controlled.

DEFINITIONS BY BEHAVIOURISTS

1. **Classical Conditioning:** It is an automatic type of learning in which a stimulus acquires the capacity to evoke a response that was originally evoked by another stimulus. - *Ivan Pavlov*
2. Learning is the process of forming associations or bonds, which he defined as "the connection of a certain act with a certain situation and resultant pleasure" - *E.L.Thorndike*

3. **Operant conditioning**: "The operant conditioning may be defined as any learning which is based on response contingent reinforcement and does not involve choice among experimentally defined alternatives"

- B.F.Skinner

THEORIES OF LEARNING

The theories of learning are divided into two broad categories (1) S-R theories and (2) cognitive field theories.

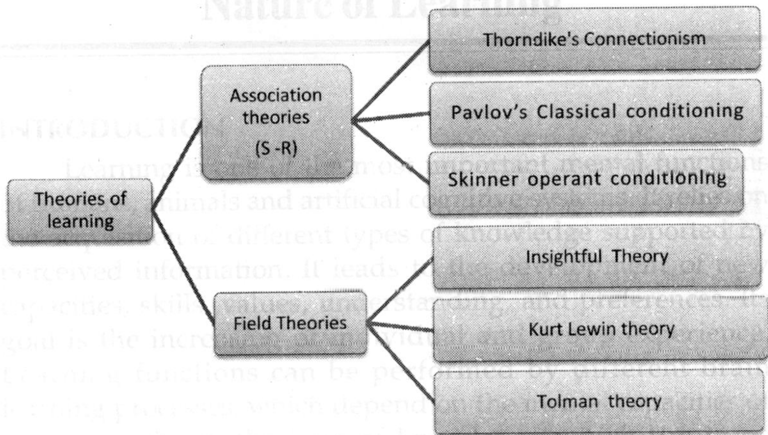

THORNDIKE'S TRIAL AND ERROR LEARNING

Edward Lee Thorndike (1874-1949) was as American Psychologist. He began his studies in psychology in Howard University. He later transferred to Columbia University where he earned his Ph.D. in psychology in 1898. Thorndike published more than 78 books and at least 400 articles before his death. He was the first to introduce the concept of reward in learning. The first psychological research concerned with associative learning was conducted by E.L.Thorndike on animals.

Experiment

Thorndike placed a hungry cat in a puzzle box and food was kept outside the box. The cat had made many trails to pull the latch to come out of the box. The cat has made several random activities jumping, dashing and moving to get out from the puzzle box.

The cat would claw, bite and scurry widely about until it accidently touched the release and cat was freed. The cat took some food which was placed outside. The cat was again placed in the box. The cat made fewer trails in touching the release. This experiment was repeated that in the number of successive trails the duration was reduced. Eventually the cat would learn to escape immediately without random actively.

LAWS OF LEARNING

Thorndike defines the following basic laws of learning:

(i) Law of Readiness

(ii) Law of Exercise

(iii) Law of Effect

(i) **Law of Readiness:** Learning requires readiness or preparedness on the part of the learner. Readiness depends on both maturation and experience of the learner. Sufficient physical and mental maturities are required for learning any type of activity.

(ii) **Law of Exercise:** The law of exercise is known as the law of habit formation. The law implies the strengthening of S-R connections with practice and their weakening when practice is not continued. So, the effect of learning is improved by continued practice. This law has two sub-laws.

- *Law of Use:* The S-R connection is strengthened by practice
- *Law of disuse:* When practice is discontinued, connection is weakened

(iii) **Law of effect:** This law is also referred to as 'Law of Satisfaction and Annoyance' or 'Reward and Punishments'. The law explains the importance of effect or consequence in strengthening and weakening of connection. If the results of learning are satisfying to the learner, learner gets stamped in. When the results are not satisfying, learning is stamped out. Satisfying results strengthen the bond between stimulus and response. Thus the law emphasizes the role of rewards and punishments in the process of learning.

PROCESS OF LEARNING

Some of the following process of learning has been included in the Thorndike theory.

1. **Drive:** Hungry cat intensified by the sight of the food.
2. **Goal:** To get food by getting out of the box.
3. **Block:** The cat was confined in the box with a closed door.
4. **Random movements:** The cat persistently tried to come out of the box without knowing how.
5. **Chance success:** Striving and random movements the cat by chance succeeded in opening the door.
6. **Selection:** Gradually cat recognized the correct way to manipulate the latch.
7. **Fixation:** At last cat learned the proper way to open the door by eliminating all the incorrect responses & fixing only the right response.

Principles of Learning based on Thorndike's Experiment

- Learning involves trial and error.
- Learning is the result of formation of connection or bonds (S-R).
- Learning is incremental not insightful.

- Learning is direct; not cognitive.
- The S-R connections are established in nervous system.
- The connection (bond) strength can be increased or decreased.

Strengths

- Motivate the child before learning.
- Make use of the previous knowledge.
- Arrange task from simple to complex and complex to simple
- Strengthen S – R connections of those things to be remembered by regular use/practice weaken others by disuse or by annoying consequences.
- Rote memory and mechanical repetition may be resorted judiciously.
- Punishment should be judiciously used.
- Provide maximum opportunity to review.
- Provide rewards, prize and praise

DEMERITS

Some of the following demerits are:

- Learning is a continuous process not discrete as Thorndike visualize
- Problem solving learning does not depend on trails and errors as Thorndike demonstration.
- Remembering and forgetting are neglected.
- Transfer of learning cannot be explained.
- Practice or exercise drill of the same thing may lead to functional fixedness and one's ability to solve problems.

EDUCATIONAL IMPLICATIONS OF THIS THEORY

Some of the important significance of:

- Adequate practice or drill should be undertaken to ensure that learning becomes stable and effective.
- Periodical review of learning material is necessary.
- Bad habits can be eliminated through disuse, leading to forgetting.

- Reward and punishments can be used better for effective learning.
- Working of arithmetical problems is done through this method.

PAVLOV'S CLASSICAL CONDITIONING THEORY

The study of classical conditioning began in the 20th century with the work of the Nobel Prize winner Russian physiologist, Ivan Pavlov. (1849-1936). He was basically interested in the studies of the glandular secretions involved in the digestive processes.

Conditioning represents learning at a lower level. A great variety of our everyday experiences are learnt through conditioning procedures. Conditioning is nothing but "the establishment of connection between a stimulus and a response which have no natural connection between them". It is learning at a very simple level, learning which we acquire mostly unconsciously. The basic principles of this learning process can be understood from the experiments of classical conditioning.

DEFINITION OF CONDITION

"Conditioning is the automatization of behaviour by repetition of stimuli which follow in giving response and which ultimately become cause for the behaviour which is formally and merely accompanied" *-H.W.Nernard*

"The most simple interpretation of this phenomenon is that when two stimuli are presented repeatedly together, the new one first then the original, effect one, the new one also become effective" *-J.P.Guilford*

PAVLOV'S EXPERIMENT

Pavlov made experiments with a hungry dog and evoked his salivary reflex by conditioning stimuli. In his experiment, kept a dog hungry for the whole night and then tied him on to the experimental table which was fitted with certain mechanically controlled devices. The dog was made comfortable and distractions were excluded as far as it was possible to do so. The observer kept himself hidden from the view of the dog but able to view the experiments by means of a set of mirrors. Arrangement was made to give food to the dog through automatic devices. Every time when the food was presented before the dog, he also arranged for the ringing of the bell. When the food was presented before the dog and the bell was rung, there was automatic secretion of saliva from the mouth of the dog. The activity of presenting the food accompanied with a ringing of the bell was repeated several times and the amount of saliva secreted was measured by cubic meter which was attached to bow of the dog.

After several trials, the dog was given no food but the bell was rung. In this case also the amount of saliva secreted was recorded and measured. It was found that even at the absence of food (natural stimulus), the ringing of the bell (an artificial stimulus) caused the dog to secrete the saliva (natural response).In this experiment, the dog learned to salivate at the sound of the bell. This kind of learning was named as Learning by Conditioning.

Pavlov and Conditioning

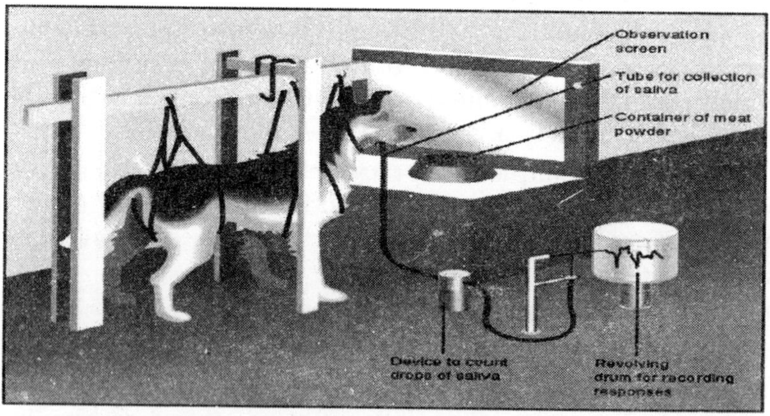

Stages of Classical Conditioning

Stage 1 (Before Conditioning)

Food (UCS) → Salivation (UCR)

Bell (CS) → No response

Stage 2 (During Conditioning)

Bell (CS) + Food (UCS) → Salivation (CR)

Stage 3 (After Conditioning)

Bell (CS) → Salivation (CR)

Some Phenomena of Classical Conditioning/Principles of Classical Conditioning

The various phenomena discovered by Pavlov in his experiment on classical conditioning are explained below:

(a) **Law of Higher Order Conditioning**

The bell sound used formally can be used to another neutral stimulus (say light). Pavlov called this as higher order conditioning. Pavlov found that higher order conditioning is possible. Pavlov found that conditioned response also occurs to CS_2 after a few trials. The trial proceeds in the following stages:

(i)	U.S (Food)	U.R (Saliva)
(ii)	C.S + U.S. (Bell+Food)	C.R (Saliva)
(iii)	C.S (Bell)	C.R (Saliva)
(iv)	$C.S._2$ + $C.S._1$ (Light+Bell)	C.R (Saliva)
(v)	$C.S._2$ (Light)	C.R (Saliva)

(b) **Law of Causation:** According to this law, a conditioned response is established by a series of contiguous pairings of CS and UCS. Best Conditioning occurs when the CS and UCS are presented simultaneously.

(c) **Law of Extinction:** The process of gradual disappearance of the conditioned response or disconnection of the S-R association is called extinction.

(d) **Law of Spontaneous recovery:** After extinction, when a conditioned response is no longer evident, the behaviour often reappears spontaneously but at a reduced intensity. The phenomenon – the reappearance of apparently extinguished conditioned response after an interval in which the pairing of conditioned stimulus (CS) and unconditioned stimulus (US) has not been repeated is called spontaneous recovery. It shows that, the learning is suppressed rather than forgotten. As the time passes, the suppression may become so strong that there would, ultimately be no further possibility of SR.

(e) **Law of generalization:** Suppose a classical conditioning (CR) is established to a bell sound, the same generalization is shown a buzzer sound also. If conditioning was established using bell as the CS, the CR will occur even for a buzzer. Ex: For a child, if fear response is obtained for a policeman, it may be obtained for anybody in Khaki uniform.

(f) **Law of discrimination:** It is the opposite of stimulus generalization. A selective classical conditioning (CR) can be established by a selective reinforcement. When the CR that follows the buzzer sound is nor reinforced, then the CR to the buzzer sound gets weakened and becomes inactive.

EDUCATIONAL SIGNIFICANCE OF THE THEORY

The important significance is:

- Developing positive attitude among students.
- Classical conditioning used in language learning associating words with pictures or meanings.
- It can be used to develop good habits in children such as cleanliness, respect for elders, punctuality etc.
- It emphasis the idea of continuity, similarity and contract as the factors of association in a learning situation.
- Montessori system is based on this theory.
- Breaking of bad habits and elimination of conditioned fear, through the use of reconditioning process.

OPERANT CONDITIONING AND SHAPING

Burrhus Frederic Skinner was born on 20th March 1904, in the small Pennsylvania town of Susquehanna. He got his master in Psychology in 1930 and his doctorate in 1931. In 1945, he became the chairman of the Psychology Department at Indiana University. On 18th August 1990, B.F.Skinner died of Leukemia. Skinner is called as father of operant conditioning.

OPERANT CONDITIONING

Learning which is due to voluntary behavior is called operant conditioning. (Operant conditioning refers to a kind of learning process where a response is made more probable or more frequent by reinforcement. It helps in the learning of operant behavior, the behavior that is not necessarily associated with a known stimulus).

EXPERIMENT

Skinner (1948) studied operant conditioning by conducting experiments using animals which he placed in a *'Skinner Box'* which was similar to Thorndike's puzzle box. With a bar and a food tray he constructed a puzzle box and drove a hungry rat into the puzzle box. The hungry rat wandered here and there and pushed the bar. The bar and the food tray had its connections. When the rat pushed the bar down a food pellet fell into the tray and it ate the food. The rat learned the task of pressing to get food needs from which we can understand that reinforcement is needed to achieve a task. Skinner at first tested this theory with rats, later he experimented the test with pigeons.

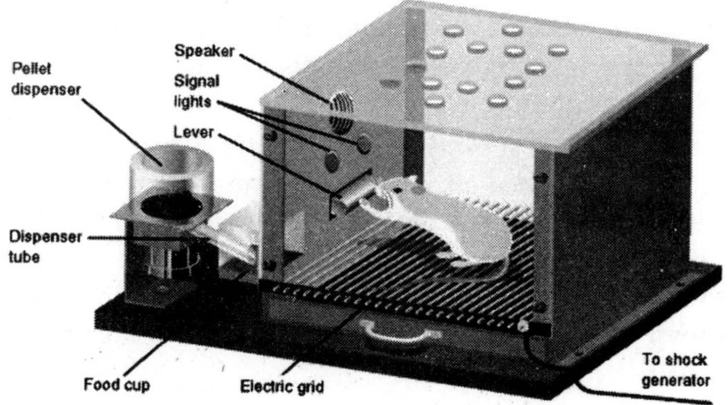

TERMS USED BY SKINNER

According to him, skinner offers two terms. That is

(a) Response

(b) Reinforcement

(a) Response

Skinner identified three types of responses or operant that can follow behavior.

- *Neutral operants:* Responses from the environment that neither increase nor decrease the probability of a behavior being repeated.
- *Reinforces:* Responses from the environment that increase the probability of a behavior being repeated. Reinforces can be either positive or negative.
- *Punishers:* Responses from the environment that decrease the likelihood of a behavior being repeated. Punishment weakens behavior.

(b) Reinforcement

Positive Reinforcement

Skinner showed how positive reinforcement worked by placing a hungry rat in his Skinner box. The box contained a lever on the side and as the rat moved about the box it would accidentally knock the lever. Immediately it did so a food pellet would drop into a container next to the lever. The rats quickly learned to go straight to the lever after a few times of being put in the box. The consequence of receiving food if they pressed the lever ensured that they would repeat the action again and again.

Positive reinforcement strengthens a behavior by providing a consequence an individual finds rewarding. For example, if the teacher gives the students Rs. 50 each time the pupils complete their homework (i.e. a reward) they will be more likely to repeat this behavior in the future, thus strengthening the behavior of completing their homework.

Negative Reinforcement

The removal of an unpleasant reinforce can also strengthen behavior. This is known as negative reinforcement because it is the removal of an adverse stimulus which is 'rewarding' to the animal or person. Negative reinforcement strengthens behavior because it stops or removes an unpleasant experience.

For example, if the students do not complete their homework, they give the teacher Rs.5. They will complete their homework to avoid paying Rs.5, thus strengthening the behavior of completing their homework.

Skinner showed how negative reinforcement worked by placing a rat in his Skinner box and then subjecting it to an unpleasant electric current which caused it some discomfort. As the rat moved about the box it would accidentally knock the lever. Immediately it did so the electric current would be switched off. The rats quickly learned to go straight to the lever after a few times of being put in the box. The consequence of escaping the electric current ensured that they would repeat the action again and again. In fact Skinner even taught the rats to avoid the electric current by turning on a light just before the electric current came on. The rats soon learned to press the lever when the light came on because they knew that this would stop the electric current being switched on.

These two learned responses are known as *Escape Learning* and *Avoidance Learning*.

PUNISHMENT (WEAKENS BEHAVIOR)

Punishment is defined as the opposite of reinforcement since it is designed to weaken or eliminate a response rather than increase it. It is an aversive event that decreases the behavior that it follows.

There are many problems with using punishment, such as:

- Punished behavior is not forgotten, it's suppressed - behavior returns when punishment is no longer present.
- Causes increased aggression - shows that aggression is a way to cope with problems.

- Creates fear that can generalize to undesirable behaviors, e.g., fear of school.
- Does not necessarily guide toward desired behavior - reinforcement tells you what to do, punishment only tells you what not to do.

BEHAVIOR SHAPING

A further important contribution made by Skinner (1951) is the notion of behaviour shaping through successive approximation. Skinner argues that the principles of operant conditioning can be used to produce extremely complex behaviour if rewards and punishments are delivered in such a way as to encourage move an organism closer and closer to the desired behaviour each time.

LAWS OF OPERANT CONDITIONING

1. Process of operant reinforcement

The operant conditioning is that, if the occurrence of an operant is followed by presentation of reinforcing stimulus the strength - probability is increased. Reinforcement has also two categories:

1. A positive reinforce is any stimulus, the presentation of which strengthens the behaviour upon which is made contingent or adding something.
2. A negative reinforce is any stimulus, the withdrawal of which strengthens that behaviour or removing something. Since in both cases responses strengthened, reinforcement is taking Place.

2. Process of operant extinction

In operant conditioning, an operant is strengthened through its reinforcement or weakened through its extinction. Extinction is the reverse of reinforcement. When a reinforcing stimulus no longer occurs following a response, the less and less frequent, this is operant extinction.

3. Process of Science behaviour

Skinner visualizes a great and crucial future for a science of behaviour. Skinner's goal in psychology is to achieve the degree of prediction and control with regard to human behaviour that has achieved by the physical sciences.

4. Process of generalization

Skinner designed some experiments and observation for studying human learning. Human beings are capable of generalizing experiences, acquired in one situation and other situations. Generalization according to him may be of two types:

(i) **Response Generalization:** It refers to the fact that when responses are repeated, they are likely to vary over the range of more or less similar acts. The principle of generalization is the one that allows the individual to get nearer to the acts.

(ii) **Stimulus Generalization:** It Occurs when a particular response elicited by a particular stimuli. Example of the principle is, a boy who has the fear with a teacher may generalize fear to other teachers.

Educational Implications

- The main contribution of theory lies in the development of new area in field of education, it has revolutionized the whole system of education by developing programmed instruction or Instruction Technology.
- Reinforcement for the right responses makes teaching learning effective.
- The immediate feedback is a key for effective learning as well as any other behaviour.
- This developed System of learning is known as programmed learning or programmed instruction.
- The school should practice the principles of operant conditioning namely to destroy the element of fear from school atmosphere by using positive reinforcement.
- Desired behaviours of students should be reinforced at once to increase the likelihood or re-occurrence of the behaviour in future.
- Each step of the behaviour is to be reinforced.

LIMITATIONS OF OPERANT CONDITIONING

The following are the limitation of skinner's theory

- He has ignored the functioning of mental structure and hereditary factors.
- The concepts or reinforcement fails to account for curiosity and creativity.
- He neglects the innate potentialities and abilities.
- The application is doubtful in normal setting for human learning.

The mental processes are not mechanical but are creative and productive.

Difference between Classical and Operant Conditioning

Classical Conditioning	Operant Conditioning
(1)	(2)
It was developed by Russian Physiologist Ivan P. Pavlov.	It was developed by B.F. Skinner
The occurrence of conditioned response(CR) is reflexively.	It is called Skinnerian or type-n learning (operant).
It is signal Conditioning.	It is instrumental Conditioning.
It is called Pavlovian or type-1 learning (Respondents). Forced by unconditioned stimulus(UCS)	The response is more voluntary and spontaneous.
The unconditioned stimulus (UCS) occurs without regard to the subject's behavior.	The reward is contingent upon the occurrence of response.
It is described as preparatory or Anticipatory response and is also called signal learning.	It serves primarily to emphasize or guide an organism which already has certain responses available in its repertoire.
The association between stimulus and response(S-R) is on the basis of law of Contiguity.	The association between stimulus and response(S-R) is on the basis of law of Effect.
It is Controlled by Autonomic Nervous System in the Organism.	It is controlled by Central Nervous System in the Organism.

(Contd...)

(1)	(2)
Bondage between Specific Unconditioned stimulus (UCS)/ Conditioned stimulus (CS) is established.	Tendency to respond in a specific manner is developed.
Reinforcement comes first as in Pavlov's experiment. Food is presented first to elicit the response.	Reinforcement is provided after the response is made by the organism.
Conditioned stimulus (CS) and Unconditioned stimulus (UCS) can be placed in different temporal sequences, close contiguity is followed.	Close contiguity is followed and S-R chain is formed.
It focuses on the single(S-R) stimulus response bondage.	It is concerned with sequence of response. A chain of responses is formed which leads to the desired goal.
It present different pictures of behavior and learning in which an arbitrary stimulus is associated with a high specific, elicit able response.	The situation describes the differentiation and Discrimination of a response out of a mass behavior in response to complex stimulus field.
The essence of learning is stimulus substitution.	The essence of learning is response modification.
The Classical Conditioned reflexes may have zero strength initially.	The operant cannot have zero strength because it has to occur at least once before it can be reinforced.
Respondent behavior is internal.	Operant is external behavior.

SOCIAL LEARNING

Social Learning Theory argues that learning occurs within social situations and contexts. Social learning theory also considers how people learn from each other and includes related concepts such as:

- observational learning
- imitation
- bahavioural modeling.

In Social learning, three variables - the person, learning Environment and modeled behaviours influence each other.

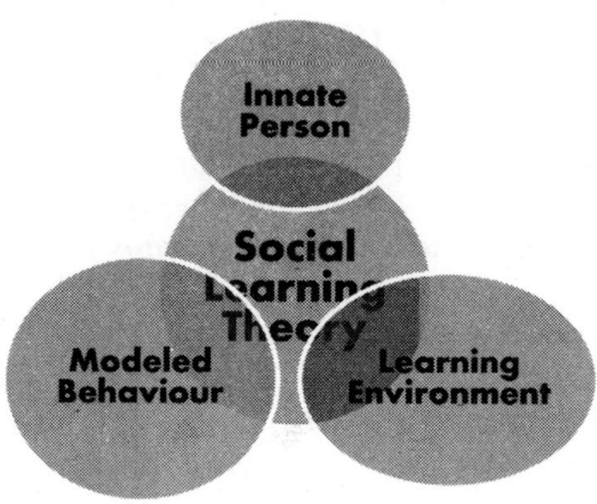

METHOD

A lab experiment was used, in which the independent variable (type of model) was manipulated in three conditions:

- Aggressive model shown to 24 children
- Non-aggressive model shown to 24 children
- No model shown (control condition) - 24 children

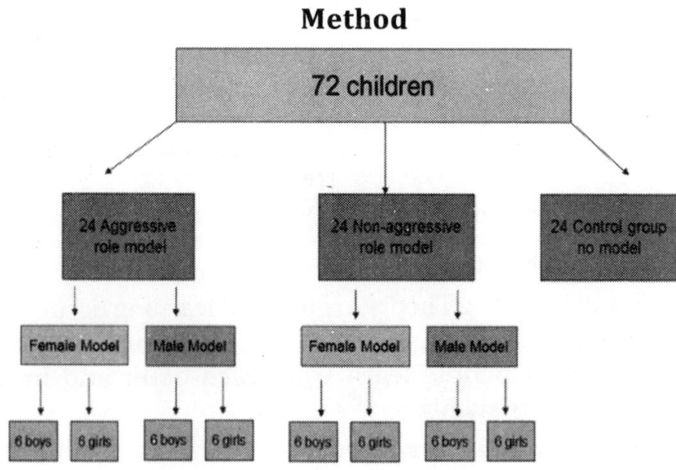

Stage 1: Modeling

In the experimental conditions children were individually shown into a room containing toys and played with some potato prints and pictures in a corner for 10 minutes while either:

1. 24 children (12 boys and 12 girls) watched a male or female model behaving aggressively towards a toy called a 'Bobo doll'. The adults attacked the Bobo doll in a distinctive manner - they used a hammer in some cases, and in others threw the doll in the air and shouted "Pow, Boom".
2. Another 24 children (12 boys and 12 girls) were exposed to a non-aggressive model that played in a quiet and subdued manner for 10 minutes (playing with a tinker toy set and ignoring the bobo-doll).
3. The final 24 children (12 boys and 12 girls) were used as a control group and not exposed to any model at all.

Stage 2: Aggression Arousal

All the children (including the control group) were subjected to 'mild aggression arousal'. Each child was (separately) taken to a room with relatively attractive toys.

As soon as the child started to play with the toys the experimenter told the child that these were the experimenter's very best toys and she had decided to reserve them for the other children.

Stage 3: Test for Delayed Imitation

The next room contained some aggressive toys and some non-aggressive toys. The non-aggressive toys included a tea set, crayons, three bears and plastic farm animals. The aggressive toys included a mallet and peg board, dart guns, and a 3 foot Bobo doll.

The child was in the room for 20 minutes and their behavior was observed and rated though a one-way mirror. Observations were made at 5-second intervals therefore giving 240 response units for each child.

Other behaviors that didn't imitate that of the model were also recorded e.g. punching the Bobo doll on the nose.

RESULTS

- Children who observed the aggressive model made far more imitative aggressive responses than those who were in the non-aggressive or control groups.
- There was more partial and non-imitative aggression among those children who has observed aggressive behavior, although the difference for non-imitative aggression was small.
- The girls in the aggressive model condition also showed more physical aggressive responses if the model was male, but more verbal aggressive responses if the model was female. However, the exception to this general pattern was the observation of how often they punched Bobo, and in this case the effects of gender were reversed.
- Boys were more likely to imitate same-sex models than girls. The evidence for girls imitating same-sex models is not strong.
- Boys imitated more physically aggressive acts than girls. There was little difference in the verbal aggression between boys and girls.

The findings support Bandura's (1977) Social Learning Theory. That is, children learn social behavior such as aggression through the process of observation learning - through watching the behavior of another person. This study has important implications for the effects of media violence on children.

PRINCIPLES OF OBSERVATION OR SOCIAL LEARNING THEORY

There are several Guiding principles behind observational learning or social learning theory:

- People learn by observing the behaviour of others and by observing the outcome of those behaviours.
- According to Social learning theorists, people are able to learn through observation.
- Cognition plays a certain role in learning. Awareness and expectations of future reinforcements or punishments have an impact on the behaviours people exhibit.
- Social Learning theory is a type of bridge or transition between behaviourist learning theories and cognitive theories.
- The observer will imitate the model's behaviour, if the model possesses characteristics. It is attributes like talent, intelligence, power, good looks or popularity that the observer finds attractive or desirable.
- The observer will react to the way the model is treated and mimic the model's behaviour. When the model's behaviour is rewarded, the observer is more likely to reproduce the rewarded behaviour. When the model is punished (an example of vicarious punishment), the observer is less likely to reproduce the same behaviour.
- A distinction exists between an observer's "acquiring" behaviour and "performing" behaviour. Through observation, the observer can acquire the behaviour without performing it. The observer may then later, in situations where is an incentive to do so, display the behaviour.

STEPS

According to Bandura (1977), the following processes or steps are usually involved in this kind of learning.

(i) ***Attending to and perceiving the behaviour:*** In this step the learner is made to observe the behaviour of the person acting as a model. Here the total behaviour or a particular aspect of it may attract and become the subject of close attention.

(ii) ***Remembering the behaviour:*** In this step, what the learner observes is filed away in his memory in the form of mental images.

(iii) ***Converting the memory into action:*** In this step, a behaviour observed and remembered by the learner is analyzed in terms of its acceptability to the learner with reference to the demands of his self and environment. It is transformed into action only afterwards and thus the observed relevant and accepted aspects of the model's behaviour are imitated by the learner.

(iv) ***Reinforcement of the imitated behaviour:*** In this final step, the behaviour of the modern imitated or the learner is reinforced for proper adoption and further continuance.

EDUCATIONAL IMPLICATIONS

Social learning theory has numerous implications for classrooms:

- Students learn a great deal simply by observing other.
- Describing the consequences of behaviour increase appropriate rewards of various behaviours.
- Modeling provides an alternative to teaching new behaviours. Instead of using shaping, an operant conditioning and modeling is a faster, more efficient the four essential conditions exist - attention, retention, motor reproduction and motivation.
- Teachers must model appropriate behaviour and take care that they do not model inappropriate behaviours.

- Teachers should expose students to a variety of models which is important to break down stereotypes.
- Students must believe that they are capable of accomplishing a task; it is important to develop a sense of self-efficacy for students. Teachers can promote such self-efficacy by making students receive confidence-building message, watch other being successful, and experience success on their own.
- Teacher should help students set realistic expectations, ensuring that expectations are realistically challenging. Sometimes a task is beyond a student's ability.
- Self-regulation techniques provide an effective method for improving student's behaviour.

STRENGTHS OF BEHAVIOURISM

The main strengths of Behaviourism are as follows:

- It can be used to formulate behavioural contracts in the school as well as at home.
- It is helpful in bringing about behaviour modification (desired outcome) with the help of reinforcement, punishment and extinction.
- Cueing responses to behaviour allow the learner to react in a predictable way under certain conditions.
- Success of outcomes is easily measurable.
- Guarantees specific learning
- Ease of application.

WEAKNESSES OF BEHAVIOURISM

The main strengths of behaviourism are as follows:

- It is an extrapolation of animal behaviour to humans.
- Behaviourism fails to explain the development of human languages.
- Effect of environment it shaping the behaviour of human, is not taken into account by the behaviourists.

IMPLICATION OF BEHAVIOURISM

- Learners should be told the explicit outcomes of the learning, so that they can set expectations and can judge for themselves, whether or not they have achieved the outcomes of the day's lesson.
- Learners must be tested to determine whether or not they have achieved the learning. Testing and assessment should be integrated into the learning sequence to check the learner's achievement level and to provide appropriate feedback.
- Learning materials must be sequenced appropriately to promote learning. The sequence could take the form of simple to complex, known to unknown, and knowledge to application.
- Learners must be provided with feedback so that they can monitor how they are doing and take corrective action if required.
- The techniques of reinforcement and punishment have been employed by the teachers in the classrooms to promote desirable behavior and discourage unwanted behavior of the learners.

PRACTICAL IMPLICATIONS OF BEHAVIOURISM

Current educational practices are influenced by behaviorist features like:

Curriculum Planning

The following list outlines curriculum-planning steps commonly undertaken by teachers at different educational levels.

- Identify the need for the programme;
- Determine the aims and instructional objectives of the programme;
- Define the characteristics of the target group;
- List the precise learning outcomes;
- Categorize learning outcomes according to Bloom's taxonomies;

- Break the material down into small units;
- Carefully sequence these units;
- Provide frequent practice to strengthen the stimulus-response bond;
- Ensure that the learner responds(does things);
- Observe and assess any behavioural changes;
- Provide opportunities for frequent learner feedback;
- Reinforce 'correct' behaviour with immediate rewards;
- Evaluate the effectiveness of the programme;
- Modify and improve the programme;

LEARNING OUTCOMES

Learning outcomes, which have developed from the behavioural educational objectives described above, are increasingly used at all levels of education, although their application is more straightforward when the behaviours are easily observed. Their use is more difficult when applied to complex and internal thought processes. A learning outcome is an explicit statement of what learner will be able to do as a result of completing a course of study. A learning outcomes statement includes:

- Action, expressed using precise behavioural verbs;
- Context, which requires reference to the conditions of performance;
- Threshold, which is an indication of acceptable performance-that is a statement about the performance threshold required.

Learning outcomes help learners at all levels to understand exactly what is expected of them and to tailor their learning activities accordingly. One of the major contributions of behaviourism to contemporary educational practice has been to remove the mystique and vagueness that has frequently characterized the discourse of educational aims and objectives.

ASSESSMENT

It is commonly held that effective assessment tasks should test the performance of behaviours stated in learning outcomes under the same conditions as those under which they were learnt. For example, if the learning outcome states that apprentices carpenters will be able to hang a door, the assessment should require them to hang a door rather than describe the technique in a written examination, which is what often happens.

Behaviourist principles are useful as part of formative assessment, which is a kind of assessment designed to provide feedback for the learner and teacher, rather than to record or certified achievement. Formative assessment may be seen as a form of reinforcement, designed to motivate and encourage learners. To be effective, the reinforcement of desired behaviour must be provided consistently and in a timely manner so that the correct response is reinforced. When it comes to assessment, therefore, learners should receive feedback as quickly as possible after the assessment task.

BAHAVIOUR MANAGEMENT

Changing or strengthening learners' behaviours is the aim of most elementary learning programmes. The strengthening of specific behaviours act as a precursor to the development of cognitive skills. As part of the process of behaviour management, teachers can use operant conditioning techniques, which Skinner claims work best in providing motivation for learning. Indeed, positive reinforcement or the use of praise as a motivator lies behind practices that seek to reward learners when they demonstrate the behaviour the teacher has set out to inculcate. Reinforcers may be:

- Material, such as prizes and awards;
- Social, such as teacher attention, approval or praise;
- Activity-related, such as an opportunity to engage in a favorite activity;
- Intrinsic, such as feeling of self – actualization or pride.

CONCLUSION

In this Unit, we have examined different theories of learning and learning approaches. Factors affecting learning like learner's cognitive abilities, previous experiences and the content of the subject determine the method of learning preferred by the learner. In order to enable the learner to learn by their own learning style, the teacher should have the knowledge of different learning theories as well as their classroom implications. The contribution of these theories had their impact on the process of teaching and learning. Each of the approaches in the learning theories has added something to the understanding of the learning process which is so complex. A thorough understanding of the different phases and various types of learning could be brought by getting a in-depth knowledge of the various approaches of the different learning theories.

QUESTIONS

1. Discuss in detail about the classical conditioning of Pavlov.
2. Explain the Trial and Error learning of Thorndike.
3. Write an essay on Bandura's social learning.
4. Write a note on the contribution of B.F Skinner to learning.
5. Discuss about concept of Behaviorism.

Cognitive and Humanistic Theories of Learning

INTRODUCTION

Learning is the central theme of education. Learning is a change in behavior for better or worse. Learning is a complex process. It is difficult to give a universally acceptable definition. Learning is a lifelong process. It begins with life and ends with life. It involves constant change, adjustment and development and skills on the one hand, modification of behavior on other hand modification measured in terms of improvement of behavior. Learning facilitates the modification of behavior in new situations.

Teaching using this theory is best done wherein the student is central and the learning is personalized. The educator's role is best suited to that of a facilitator. Cognitive learning, a highly active process largely directed by the individual, involves perceiving the information, interpreting it based on what is already known, and then reorganizing the information into new insights or understanding (Bandura, 2001; Hunt, Ellis, & Ellis, 2004). Cognitive theorists, unlike behaviorists, maintain that reward is not necessary for learning. More important are learners' goals and expectations, which create disequilibrium, imbalance, and tension that motivate them to act. Educators trying to influence the learning process must recognize the variety of past experiences, perceptions, ways of incorporating and thinking about information, and diverse aspirations, expectations, and social influences that affect any learning situation.

The Humanist Learning Theory strives to address the learner's personal development. Learning is "...from the perspective of the human potential for growth." The humanist's standpoint is that we (humans) control our own destiny, we're inherently good and have the best intentions to improve our world for ourselves and others, our paths and goals are our choice, and we possess unlimited potential for growth and development. To that end, the teacher should provide a positive learning environment in which the student is comfortable (emotionally) and strive to build the student's self-esteem and confidence, the student's desire to learn, and allow the student to learn at his/her own pace and direction. Experiential learning is one of the key aspects of this learning theory – incorporating the student's own history and experience to build upon and guide their current learning.

MEANING OF LEARNING

The knowledge we acquire, the language we speak, the habits, attitudes and skills development in us are all due to learning. Psychologists define learning as *"a relatively permanent training, practice or experience"*, this definition of learning has three important elements:

- Learning results in change in behavior.
- It is change that takes place through practice or experience. (Changes due to growth and maturation are relatively independent of activity, practice or experience and hence they are not learning.)
- Before it can be called learning, the change must be relatively permanent. It must last a fairly long time. But behavior changes brought about by fatigue, drugs, illness, warm up, etc. are transitory in nature and hence they are not included under learning.

DEFINITION OF LEARNING

"Learning is not acquiring knowledge or skill by mere mechanical repetitions. It is a process in which the learner organizes different elements and experiences to reach a particular goal". *- Skinner*

"Learning is the process by which an organism in satisfying its motivation adopts and adjusts its behavior in order to overcome abstracts or barriers". *- Kingly and Gray*

"Psychology of learning" says the ability to learn, that is to respond differently to a situation because of part response to the situation" *- Guthrie*

COGNITIVE PERSPECTIVES OF LEARNING

We learnt the behaviorists' perspectives of learning and the theories supporting its insights. The next perspective of educational psychology is the cognitive perspective. Cognitive psychology is the theoretical perspective that focuses on learning based on how people perceive, remember, think, speak, and problem solve. The cognitive perspective differs from the behaviorist perspective into two distinct ways. First cognitive psychology acknowledges the existence of internal mental states discharged by behaviorist. Examples of these states are belief, desire, ideas and motivation (non-observable states). Second cognitive psychologist claim memory structures determine how information is perceived, processed, stored, retrieved and forgotten. Cognitive psychology encompasses perception, categorization, memory, knowledge representation, language and thinking process.

HUMANIST PERSPECTIVES OF LEARNING

Humanistic "theories" of learning tend to be highly value – driven and hence more like prescriptions (about what ought to happen) rather than descriptions (of what does happen). The school is particularly associated with Carl Rogers, Abraham Maslow, John Holt and Malcolm they emphasize the "natural desire" of everyone to learn. Whether this natural desire is to learn whatever it is you are teaching, however, is not clear.

- It follows from this, they maintain, that learners need to be empowered and to have control over the learning process.
- So the teacher relinquishes a great deal of authority and becomes facilitators.

INSIGHT LEARNING – KOHLER

This theory is related to the cognitive type of theory of learning. It was developed by Gestalt psychologist. The main exponents are Wolfgang Kohler, Kurt Koffka and Max Wertheimer.

This theory advocates that when a particular situation is being learnt, it does not help to learn it in parts but it helps to learn its whole. Learning is an exploratory, purposive and creative activity but not a trial and error method of activity. Learning means, 'Reorganization of the perceptual field". Learning is dependent upon intelligence of the individuals.

LIFE SKETCH OF KOHLER

Kohler was born on 21st January, 1887 in the port city of Reval (now Tallinn), Governorate of Estonia, Russian Empire. His family was of German origin, and shortly after his birth they moved back to that country. There raised in a setting of teachers, nurses and other scholars he developed lifelong interests in the science as well as the arts and especially in music. In the course of his University Education he studied at the University of Tubingen (1905-06), the University of Bonn (1906-07) and the University of Berlin (1907-09). In completing his Ph.D. for which his dissertation addressed certain aspects of psychoacoustics. In 1910-13, he was an assistant at the Psychological Institute in Franfurt in which he worked with fellow psychologists; Max Wertheimer and Kurt Koffka. He immigrated to US in 1935. And he died on 11th June 1967 in Enfield, New Hampshire.

KOHLER'S EXPERIMENTS

In order to establish the existence of insight, Kohler conducted a number of experiments on a chimpanzee named Sultan. Although he conducted a number of other experiments on dogs, hens, and other creatures, his experiments with Sultan were the most noteworthy. Kohler divided his experiment into four steps.

- Sultan was placed in a cage. A stick was placed in the cage and a banana just outside the cage, but Sultan did not reach the banana. Sultan made many attempts to obtain the banana but it failed. It sat down in despair. But, after sometime it suddenly got up, lifted the stick and used it to draw the banana towards itself.
- In the second stage, Kohler placed inside the cage two sticks which could be joined to each other. This time the banana was so placed that it could not be drown by the chimpanzee towards itself with a single stick. After numerous attempts, Sultan joined the two sticks together and succeeded in obtaining the banana.
- In the third step, Kohler hung the banana from the roof of the cage of such a height as to ensure that Sultan could not reach it even by jumping upwards. A box was also placed inside the cage. After many attempts, Sultan climbed up on the box and obtained the bananas.
- In the final step, Kohler placed two boxes at one place in the cage the banana was placed at an even high level. At first, Sultan kept on trying to reach the banana by standing up on one box, but after numerous failures, it placed one box upon the other and claiming quit obtained the banana.

FACTORS INFLUENCING INSIGHT

Many experiments have thrown light upon and established the various factors which influence insight. Some of them are mentioned below:

1. Experience

Past experiences help in the insightful solution of the problems. A child cannot solve the problems of Modern Mathematics unless he is well acquainted with its symbolic language.

2. Intelligence

Insightful solution depends upon the basic intelligence of the learner. The more intelligent the individual is the greater will be his insight.

3. Learning Situation

How insightfully the organism will react depends upon the situation in which he has to act. Some situations are more favorable than the others for insightful solution. As a common observation, insight occurs when the learning situation is so arranged that all the necessary aspects are open for observation.

4. Initial Efforts or Trial and Error

Insightful learning has to pass through the process of trial and error. Whatever an activity may be, attempts or efforts or trials always lie at its root. This opens the way for insightful learning.

5. Repetition and Generalization

After having an insightful solution of a particular type of problem, the organism tries to repeat it in another situation, demanding similar type of solution. The way found in one situation helps him to react insightfully in the other identical situations.

PRINCIPLES INVOLVED IN INSIGHTFUL LEARNING

The followings are the principles involved in perceptual organization or insightful learning. Some of the basic laws propounded by Gestalt psychologists are as follows:

Law of Figure Ground

Everything is perceived in the context of its background. Thus, close relationship is there between figure and ground. For example, we try to solve a sum by using the means that closed areas are more stable and satisfying than the unclosed ones. Closed areas form groups very easily. This law is also called law of closure.

Law of Pragnanz

An organism is motivated to learn when there is tension or disequilibrium of forces in the psychological field. Learning is the removal of this tension. When we perceive an object, we find some gaps in our perceptions. These gaps are filled by the perceiver and a whole figure is prepared.

Law of Continuity

Objects having continuity are learnt easily because they can easily make a whole.

Law of Similarity

This law makes the individual to grasp things which are similar. They are picked out as they were from the total context. Similar ideas and experiences get associated. An object revives another object which resembles or looks similar to it. For example, seeing a man and remembering an intimate friend by some resemblance though never saw them together in the past.

Law of Proximity

This law states the proximate or near together things are picked up first and learnt easily than distant things. In other words, perceptual grounds are favored according to the nearness of their respective parts. Items tend to form groups if they are spaced together. For instance, a triangle or a circle is understood in this way.

Educational Implications

- Subject matter (learning material) should be presented in Gestalt form. The plant or flower as a whole be presented before the students and later on the parts should be emphasized.
- In the organization of the syllabus and planning of the curriculum, the Gestalt principle should be given due consideration. A particular subject should not be treated as the mere collection of isolated facts or topics. It should be closely integrated into a whole. Similarly the curriculum should reflect unity and cohesiveness.

- This theory has brought motivation in the fore-front by assigning purpose and motive, the central role in learning process. It is goal oriented. Purpose or goals of learning should be made clear to the students, before the teacher starts teaching.
- The greater contribution of the insight theory of learning is that it has made learning an intelligent task requiring mental abilities. It has called a halt to the age old mechanical memorization, drill and practice work which lack in basic understanding and use of thinking, reasoning and creative mental powers.
- If the teacher believes in the theory of insight learning he seeks, to overcome impatience as the moment of insight is unpredictable and sudden. He must give his students a chance to fumble and search for the solution. This fumbling and search is more than trial and error procedure. It is purposeful experimentation. It is a goal directed activity.
- The teacher must realize the necessity of preliminary steps of experimentation and purposeful search so that the child may become capable of understanding or perceiving cause and effect relationships.
- As an arrangement of the elements in the situation conditions insight, the teacher determines the methods and order of presentation that will prove most helpful.
- As insight depends upon capacity, all pupils are not able to use insight in an equal measure. The teacher recognizes differences in capacity and age and understands classroom implications of readiness.
- The function of the teacher is the teaching learning situation to help the child to perceive the goal and the intervening obstacles. If the goal is too difficult in terms of the pupil's present development, it must be made easier or its pursuit may be delayed. In a situation, where an obstacle blocks the perception or achievement of the goal. The teacher may take the following three steps:

(a) Allow the pupil to grow by waiting or by providing preparatory experiences and knowledge that will increase his power.

(b) Make the problem less difficult. Get easier text-books. Use more immediate goals. Find more concrete problems.

(c) Give the pupil some help, offer suggestions, hints, clues, show him how to take specific steps and arrange sequential approach.

Criticism

Some of the main objections against the Gestalt theory are the following;

- Gestalt is a composite of Psychology and Philosophy of Education.
- Every kind of learning for example; reading, writing, speaking etc., cannot be satisfactorily explained by the laws of Gestalt.
- Some scholars opine that the insight inherent in gestalt cannot be ascribed to children and animals because they lack power of thought. However it is often observed in daily life that even very young infants display insight in many of their activities.
- Trial and error is an essential element in gestalt at one stage or the other.

MODES OF COGNITIVE DEVELOPMENT - BRUNER

Cognitive psychologist Jerome Bruner felt the goal of education should be intellectual development, as opposed to rote memorization of facts. Bruner's theory of development and his three modes of representation. We will also explore his beliefs on learning, language, and discovery and differentiate his views from those of Jean Piaget.

Bruner held the following beliefs regarding learning and education:

- He believed curriculum should foster the development of problem-solving skills through the processes of inquiry and discovery.

- He believed that subject matter should be represented in terms of the child's way of viewing the world.
- That curriculum should be designed so that the mastery of skills leads to the mastery of still more powerful ones.
- He also advocated teaching by organizing concepts and learning by discovery.
- Finally, he believed culture should shape notions through which people organize their views of themselves and others and the world in which they live.

Three Modes of Representation

- Enactive representation (action-based)
- Iconic representation (image-based)
- Symbolic representation (language-based)

Modes of representation are the way in which information or knowledge are stored and encoded in memory. Rather than neat age related stages (like Piaget), the modes of representation are integrated and only loosely sequential as they "translate" into each other.

Enactive (0 - 1 years)

This appears first. It involves encoding action based information and storing it in our memory. For example, in the form of movement as a muscle memory, a baby might remember the action of shaking a rattle.

The child represents past events through motor responses, i.e. an infant will "shake a rattle" which has just been removed or dropped, as if the movements themselves are expected to produce the accustomed sound. And this is not just limited to children. Many adults can perform a variety of motor tasks (typing, sewing a shirt, operating a lawn mover) that they would find difficult to describe in iconic (picture) or symbolic (word) form.

Iconic (1 - 6 years)

This is where information is stored visually in the form of images (a mental picture in the mind's eye). For some, this is conscious; others say they don't experience it. This may explain why, when we are learning a new subject, it is often helpful to have diagrams or illustrations to accompany verbal information.

Symbolic (7 years onwards)

This develops last. This is where information is stored in the form of a code or symbol, such as language. This is the most adaptable form of representation, for actions & images have a fixed relation to that which they represent. Dog is a symbolic representation of a single class.

Symbols are flexible in that they can be manipulated, ordered, classified etc., so the user isn't constrained by actions or images. In the symbolic stage, knowledge is stored primarily as words, mathematical symbols, or in other symbol systems.

Bruner's constructivist theory suggests it is effective when faced with new material to follow a progression from enactive to iconic to symbolic representation; this holds true even for adult learners. A true instructional designer, Bruner's work also suggests that a learner even of a very young age is capable of learning any material so long as the instruction is organized appropriately, in sharp contrast to the beliefs of Piaget and other stage theorists.

THE IMPORTANCE OF LANGUAGE

Language is important for the increased ability to deal with abstract concepts. Bruner argues that language can code stimuli and free an individual from the constraints of dealing only with appearances, to provide a more complex yet flexible cognition. The use of words can aid the development of the concepts they represent and can remove the constraints of the "here & now" concept. Basically, he sees the infant as an intelligent & active problem solver from birth, with intellectual abilities basically similar to those of the mature adult.

Classroom Implications

- Actively engages students learning process
- Motivates students to participates
- Encourages autonomy and independence

- Promotes the development of creativity and problem – solving skills
- Provides an individualized learning experience.

STAGES OF INTELLECTUAL DEVELOPMENT – PIAGET

The most influent exponent of cognitivism was Swiss child psychologist Jean Piaget. Piaget rejected the idea that learning was the passive assimilation of given knowledge. Instead, he proposed that learning is a dynamic process comprising successive stages of adoption to reality during which learners actively construct knowledge by creating and testing their own theories of the world.

THEORY

Piaget's theory has two major parts: an "ages and stages" component that predicts what children can and cannot understand at different ages and a theory of development that describes how children develop cognitive abilities. It is the theory of development that will be the focus here because it is the major foundation for cognitive constructivist approaches to teaching and learning.

Piaget's theory of cognitive development proposes that humans cannot be "given" information which they immediately understand and use. Instead, humans must "construct" their own knowledge. They build their knowledge through experience. Experiences enable them to create "Schemas"- mental models in their heads. The schemas are the representation in the mind of a set of perceptions, ideas and actions which go together. These schemas are changed, enlarged and made more sophisticated through two complimentary processes given below:

(i) **Assimilation**: The process by which a person takes material into their mind from the environment, which may mean changing the evidence of their senses to make fit.

(ii) **Accommodation:** The difference made to one's mind or concepts by the process of assimilation.

The basic principle underlying Piaget's theory is the principle of equilibration:

All cognitive development including both intellectual and affective development progresses towards increasingly complex and stable levels of organization. Equilibration takes places through a process of adoption, That is, assimilation of new information to existing cognitive structures.

For example, learners who already have the cognitive structures necessary to solve percentage problems in mathematics will have some of the structures necessary to solve-time-rate-distance problems, but they will need to modify their existing structures to accommodate the newly acquired information to solve the new type of problem. Thus, learners adapt and develop by assimilating and accommodating new information into existing cognitive structure. It should be noted that assimilation accommodation goes together.Piaget suggested that there are four main stages in the cognitive development of children as follows,

(i) The Sensory motor stage (0 - 2 years)

(ii) The Preoperational stage (2 to 7 years)

(iii) The Concrete Operational stage (7 to 11 years)

(iv) The Formal Operational stage (11 years and above)

(i) The Sensory motor stage (0-2 years)

In the first two years, children pass through a sensory motor stage during which they progress from cognitive structures dominated by instinctual drives and undifferentiated emotions to more organized systems of concrete concepts, differentiated emotions, and their first external affective fixations. At this stage, children's outlook is essentially egocentric in the sense that they are unable to take into account other's point of view.

This stage is characterized by:

- The development of sensory, motor and perceptual skills.
- Coordination of motor activities.

- The development of rudimentary memory
- Gradual progression from reflex behavior to intentional behavior
- Development of curiosity, and trial and error exploration of immediate surroundings;
- Able to differentiate itself from objects and this is the basis of self-concept.

(ii) The Pre-operational stage (2 to 7 years)

The second stage of development lasts until around seven years of age. Children begin to use language to make sense of reality. They learn to classify objects using different criteria and to manipulate numbers. Children's increasing linguistic skills open the way for greater socialization of action and communication with others.

(iii) The Concrete Operational stage (7 to 11 Years)

Children at this point of development begin to think more logically, but their thinking can also be very rigid. They tend to struggle with abstract and hypothetical concepts. At this point, children also become less egocentric and begin to think about how other people might think and feel. They begin to understand that their thoughts are unique to them and that not everyone else necessarily shares their thoughts, feelings and opinions.

(iv) The Formal Operational stage (11 Years and above)

From the age of twelve to adolescent, the final stage of Piaget's theory involves an increase in logic, the ability to use deductive reasoning and an understanding of abstract ideas. At this point, people become capable of seeing multiple potential solutions to problems and think more scientifically about the world around them.

Educational Implications

- Focus on the process of children's thinking, not just its products.
- Recognition of the crucial role of children's self-initiated, active involvement in learning activities.

- Emphasis on practices aimed at making children adult like in their thinking
- Acceptance of individual differences in developmental process.
- Co-curricular activities have equal importance as that of curricular experiences in the cognitive development of children.
- Arrange classroom activities so that they assist and encourage self-learning.
- Curriculum should provide specific educational experience based on children's development level.
- Moral and intellectual growth goes together and only after the age of 11, can the child evaluate actions in the light of motives.
- Activity approach at the primary classes and concrete methods of illustration (like use of aids, demonstrations, etc.) at the middle school level are advocated. Verbal method of teaching should be practiced only from high school classes.

LEARNING STYLES – KOLB

David A. Kolb (born 1939) is an American educational theorist whose interests and publications focus on experiential learning, the individual and social change, career development, and executive and professional education. He is the founder and chairman of Experience Based Learning Systems (EBLS), and a Professor of Organizational Behavior in the Weather head School of Management, Case Western Reserve University.

Kolb's experiential learning theory works on two levels:

1. Four stage cycle of learning.
2. Four separate learning styles.

1. The Experiential Learning Cycle

Kolb's experiential learning style theory is typically represented by a four stage learning cycle.

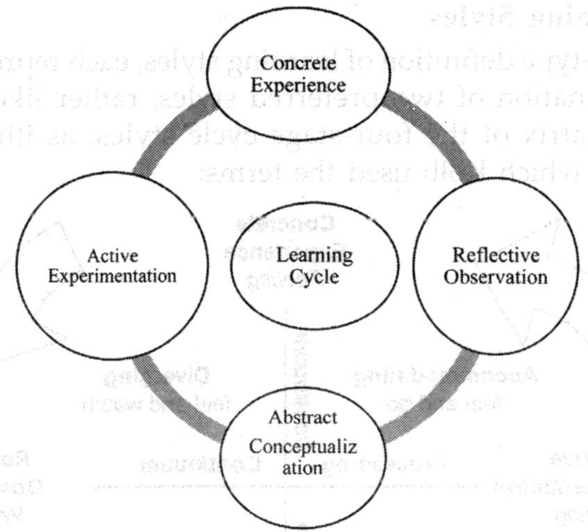

1. Concrete Experience – (CE - feelings, Kinesthetic responses)
2. Reflective Observation – (RO - watching, analyzing)
3. Abstract Conceptualization – (AC - Critical thinking)
4. Active Experimentation – (AE - Doing)

- **Concrete Experience** likes to learn by experiencing. They like games and role playing. They learn from and with other people and value discussion and feedback.
- **Reflective Observers** learn by reflecting. They like to look at things carefully from a variety of perspectives. They enjoy lectures and objective test where knowledge is demonstrated.
- **Abstract Conceptualizers** are logical and systematic. They appreciate deductive thinking based on their careful understanding. They like theory and appreciate alone study time. They create ideas that are clear and well structured.
- **Active Experimentation** learns by doing. They like to practice and try new things. They are not afraid of taking risks and are known for getting things done. They appreciate small group discussions and individual self-paced projects or activities.

2. Learning Styles

Four-type definition of learning styles, each representing the combination of two preferred styles, rather like a two-by-two matrix of the four-stage cycle styles, as illustrated below for which Kolb used the terms:

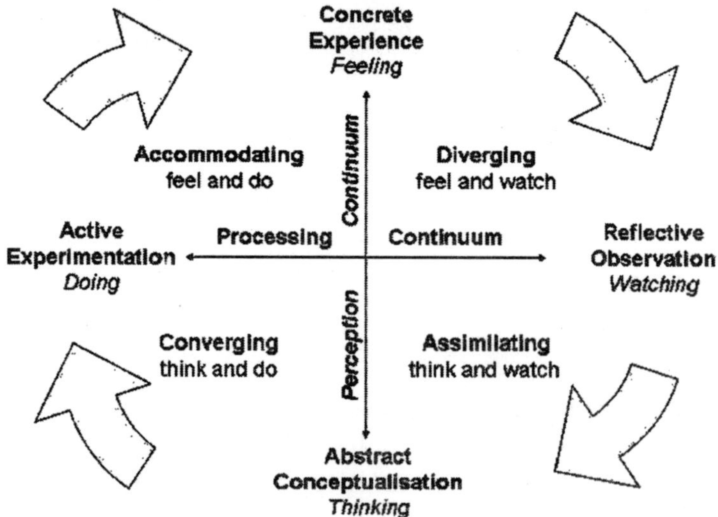

- Diverging (CE/RO)
- Assimilating (AC/RO)
- Converging (AC/AE)
- Accommodating (CE/AE)

Learning Styles Descriptions

- **Diverging (feeling and watching - CE/RO)** - These people are able to look at things from different perspectives. They are sensitive. They prefer to watch rather than do, tending to gather information and use imagination to solve problems. They are best at viewing concrete situations several different viewpoints. Kolb called this style 'Diverging' because these people perform better in situations that require ideas-generation, for example, brainstorming. People with a Diverging learning style have broad cultural interests and like to gather information. They are interested in people, tend to be imaginative and emotional, and tend to be strong in the arts. People with the Diverging style prefer to work in groups, to listen with an open mind and to receive personal feedback.

- **Assimilating (watching and thinking - AC/RO)** - The Assimilating learning preference is for a concise, logical approach. Ideas and concepts are more important than people. These people require good clear explanation rather than practical opportunity. They excel at understanding wide-ranging information and organizing it a clear logical format. People with an Assimilating learning style are less focused on people and more interested in ideas and abstract concepts. People with this style are more attracted to logically sound theories than approaches based on practical value. These learning style people are important for effectiveness in information and science careers. In formal learning situations, people with this style prefer readings, lectures, exploring analytical models, and having time to think things through.
- **Converging (doing and thinking - AC/AE)** - People with a Converging learning style can solve problems and will use their learning to find solutions to practical issues. They prefer technical tasks, and are less concerned with people and interpersonal aspects. People with a Converging learning style are best at finding practical uses for ideas and theories. They can solve problems and make decisions by finding solutions to questions and problems. People with a Converging learning style are more attracted to technical tasks and problems than social or interpersonal issues. A Converging learning style enables specialist and technology abilities. People with a Converging style like to experiment with new ideas, to simulate, and to work with practical applications.
- **Accommodating (doing and feeling - CE/AE)** - The Accommodating learning style is 'hands-on', and relies

on intuition rather than logic. These people use other people's analysis, and prefer to take a practical, experiential approach. They are attracted to new challenges and experiences, and to carrying out plans. They commonly act on 'gut' instinct rather than logical analysis. People with an Accommodating learning style will tend to rely on others for information than carry out their own analysis. This learning style is prevalent and useful in roles requiring action and initiative. People with an Accommodating learning style prefer to work in teams to complete tasks. They set targets and actively work in the field trying different ways to achieve an objective.

EDUCATIONAL IMPLICATIONS

Kolb's (1984) learning stages and cycle could be used by teachers:

- To critically evaluate the learning provision typically available to students, and to develop more appropriate learning opportunities.
- Educators should ensure that activities are designed and carried out in ways that offer each learner the chance to engage in the manner that suits them best.
- Individuals can be helped to learn more effectively by the identification of their lesser preferred learning styles and the strengthening of these through the application of the experiential learning cycle.
- Activities and material should be developed in ways that draw on abilities from each stage of the experiential learning cycle and take the students through the whole process in sequence.

SELF-ACTUALIZATION (MASLOW)

Abraham Maslow was the American psychologist. He was born on April 1, 1908 and died on June 8, 1970. He was developed the Hierarchy of Needs model in 1940-50s, and the Hierarchy of Needs theory remains valid today for understanding human motivation, management training, and personal development.

Maslow (1943) stated that people are motivated to achieve certain needs, and that some needs take precedence over others.

Hierarchy of Needs

It is important to note that Maslow's (1943, 1954) five-stage model has been expanded to include cognitive and aesthetic needs (Maslow, 1970a) and later transcendence needs (Maslow, 1970b). Changes to the original five-stage model are highlighted and include a seven-stage model and an eight-stage model; both developed during the 1960's and 1970s.

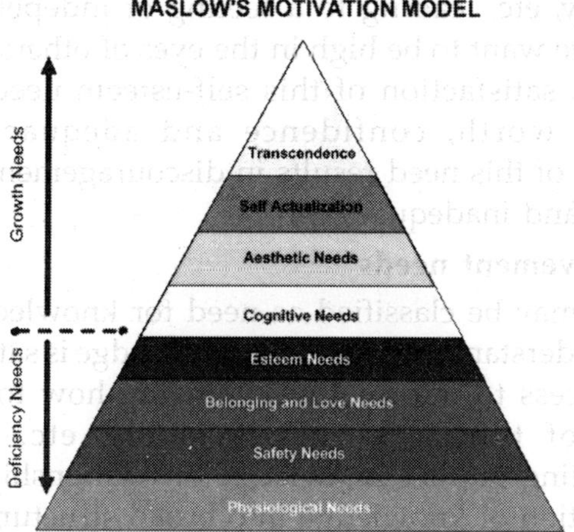

(i) Physiological needs

These are the lower in the motivational hierarchy, which include need for food, water, oxygen, sleep, sex, sensory satisfaction and the like. These are vital for survival and hence should be fulfilled before the next higher order motives become prominent. Perhaps the main reason why disadvantaged and poor children refuse to be motivated in the classroom to learn is that their basic bodily needs remain unsatisfied.

(ii) Safety and Security needs

They include shelter, clothing and personal safety, security of the future, routine, regularity, etc. Children do need discipline within their levels of understanding in order to perceive an orderly and organized world.

(iii) Affiliational needs

It refers to the individual's hunger for affection. "A pupil, who is not loveable because of his behavior, needs to be loved most". Identity implies belongingness and often underachievement of certain pupil's results from lack of love and belonging.

(iv) Esteem needs

In all of us there is a desire for strength, mastery, competency, etc. leading to a feeling of independence and freedom. We want to be high in the eyes of others. According to Maslow, satisfaction of this self-esteem need generates feeling of worth, confidence and adequacy. Lack of satisfaction of this need results in discouragement, feeling of inferiority and inadequacy.

(v) Achievement needs

They may be classified as need for knowledge and the need for understanding. Need for knowledge is satisfied when there is access to information, knowing how to do things, meaning of things, events, symbols, etc. Needs for understanding implies knowledge of relationships, process, the integration of knowledge into broad structure, etc. Thus achievement needs are related to intellectual domination and cognitive competencies.

(vi) Aesthetic needs

This is concerned with appreciation of order and beauty. One whose lower order are fully satisfied or known that he need not bother about them, derives pleasure in beauty, nature, etc. Tagore, Wordsworth, etc. are the best examples for this.

(vii) Self-actualization needs

Self actualization means to fulfill one's individual nature in all its aspects. One who is talented in one specific area feels uneasy, if that talent is not nurtured and utilized. He wants to attain perfection in that area. The highest level of functioning occurs when a person is self-actualized. People can be motivated towards self-actualization only when the lower order needs are satisfied.

(viii) Self-transcendence needs

What is less well-known is that Maslow amended his model near the end of his life, and so the conventional portrayal of his hierarchy is incomplete. In his later thinking he argued that there is another, higher level of development, what he called self-transcendence. We achieve this level by focusing on goals beyond the self like altruism, spiritual awakening, liberation from egocentricity, and ultimately the unity of being. Here is how he put it:

Transcendence refers to the very highest and most inclusive or holistic levels of human consciousness, behaving and relating, as ends rather than means, to oneself, to significant others, to human beings in general, to other species, to nature and to the cosmos.

SELF-ACTUALIZATION

Psychologist Abraham Maslow stated that human motivation is based on people seeking fulfillment and change through personal growth. Self-actualized people are those who were fulfilled and doing all they were capable of. And he believed self-actualization could be measured through the concept of peak experiences. This occurs when a person experiences the world totally for what it is, and there are feelings of euphoria, joy and wonder.

Self-actualization is the feeling that you have arrived. It comes with a desire to learn what you are good at and do your best at everything. The achievement of one's full potential through creativity, independence, spontaneity, and a grasp of the real world. The process of establishing oneself as a whole person, able to develop one's abilities and to understand oneself.

DEFINITION OF SELF-ACTUALIZATION

"It refers to the person's desire for self-fulfillment, namely, to the tendency for him to become actualized in what he is potentially" - *Maslow*

"It is important to note that self-actualization is a continual process of becoming rather than a perfect state one reaches of a 'happy ever after" - *Hoffman*

Characteristics of self-actualizers:

- **Problem Centering:** The self-actualizing person is someone who is generally strongly focused on problems outside of themselves. They are concerned with the problems of others and the problems of society.
- **Perception of reality:** The most universal characteristic of these superior people is their unusual ability to perceive other people correctly and efficiently, to see reality as it is, rather than as they wish it to be. They have a better perception of reality and more comfortable relations with it. They do not allow their desires and hopes to distort their observation.
- **Democratic Character structure:** Self-actualized people are said to be democratic. They are able to be friendly with anyone no matter what their background, class or beliefs are. They believe it is possible to learn something from everyone.
- **Acceptance of self, others, and nature:** Self-actualized accept themselves as they are, and are not ashamed or guilty about their human nature, with its shortcoming, imperfections, and weaknesses. They are also able to accept others in the same without trying to control them or perfect them in any way.
- **Spontaneous:** Self-actualized people are spontaneous, simple and natural. In other words, this kind of person is not concerned with being as others think they should be. They are individuals who are able to do what feels good and natural, simply because that is how they feel.
- **Imperfections:** Self-actualizing people are individuals who are aware of the fact that they are not perfect, that they are as human as the next person, and that there are constantly new things to learn and new ways to grow.

- **Autonomous:** The self-actualizing person is autonomous, meaning they are capable of doing things for themselves and making decisions on their own. They are strong enough to be independent of the good opinions of others.
- **Interpersonal relationship:** Self-actualizing people have deep interpersonal relationship with others. These relationships are more likely to be with others who are also self-actualized.
- **Creativeness:** Self-actualizing people are capable of being highly creative. Creativeness can be expressed in many dimensions by writing, speaking, playing, fantasies, or whatever, but self-actualizing do have moods of being creative.

Behavior leading to self-actualization:

- Experiencing life like a child, with full absorption and concentration;
- Trying new things instead of sticking to safe paths;
- Listening to your own feelings in evaluating experiences instead of the voice of tradition, authority or the majority;
- Avoiding pretense ('game playing') and being honest;
- Being prepared to be unpopular if your views do not coincide with those of the majority;
- Taking responsibility and working hard;
- Trying to identify your defenses and having the courage to give them up.

Educational Implications

The major educational implications by the Maslow theory are:

- It has contribution to teaching and classroom management in schools.
- It helps the students at the entire physical, emotional, social, and intellectual qualities and how they impact on learning.

- Student's cognitive needs can be meet by the teachers
- Students need to feel emotionally and physically safe and accepted within the classroom to progress and reach their full potential.
- Maslow suggests students must be shown that they are valued and respected in the classroom and the teacher should create a supportive environment.
- Students' self-esteem is strengthened.

THEORY OF A FULLY FUNCTIONING PERSON – CARL ROGERS

Carl Rogers (1902-1987) was a prominent psychologist and one of the founding members of the humanist movement. Rogers believed that every person could achieve their goals, wishes, and desires in life. When they did so self-actualization took place. For Rogers (1961) people who are able be self-actualizes, and that is not all of us, are called fully functioning persons. This means that the person is in touch with the here and now, his or her subjective experiences and feelings, continually growing and changing. In many ways Rogers regarded the fully functioning person as an ideal and perfect man.

1. **Rogers identified five characteristics of the fully functioning person**
   - **Open to experience:** both positive and negative emotions accepted. Negative feelings are not denied, but worked through (rather than resorting to ego defense mechanisms).
   - **Existential living:** in touch with different experiences as they occur in life, avoiding prejudging and preconceptions. Being able to live and fully appreciate the present, not always looking back to the past or forward to the future.
   - **Trust feelings:** feeling, instincts and gut-reactions are paid attention to and trusted. People's own decisions are the right ones and we should trust ourselves to make the right choices.

- **Creativity:** Creative thinking and risk taking are features of a person's life. A person does not play safe all the time. This involves the ability to adjust and change and seek new experiences.
- **Fulfilled life:** Person is happy and satisfied with life, and always looking for new challenges and experiences. For Rogers, fully functioning people are well adjusted, well balanced and interesting to know. Often such people are high achievers in society.

2. Personality Development

Central to Rogers' personality theory is the notion of self or self-concept. This is defined as "the organized, consistent set of perceptions and beliefs about oneself". The self is the humanistic term for who we really are as a person. The self is our inner personality, and can be likened to the soul, or Freud's psyche. The self is influenced by the experiences a person has in their life, and out interpretations of those experiences. Two primary sources that influence our self-concept are childhood experiences and evaluation by others.

According to Rogers (1959), we want to feel, experience and behave in ways which are consistent with our self-image and which reflect what we would like to be like, our idealself. The humanistic approach states that the self is composed of concepts unique to us. The self-concept includes three components:

(i) **Self-worth (or self-esteem)** – what we think about ourselves. Rogers believed feelings of self-worth developed in early childhood and were formed from the interaction of the child with the mother and father.

(ii) **Self-image** – How we see ourselves, which is important to good psychological health. Self-image includes the influence of our body image on inner personality. At a simple level, we might perceive ourselves as a good or bad person, beautiful or ugly. Self-image has an effect on how a person thinks feels and behaves in the world.

(iii) **Ideal self** – This is the person who we would like to be. It consists of our goals and ambitions in life, and is dynamic. The ideal self in childhood is not the ideal self in our teens or late twenties etc.

3. Self-Worth and Positive Regard

Self-worth may be seen as a continuum from very high to very low. For Carl Rogers (1959) a person who has high self-worth, that is, has confidence and positive feelings about him or she, faces challenges in life, accepts failure and unhappiness at times, and is open with people. A person with low self-worth may avoid challenges in life, not accept that life can be painful and unhappy at times, and will be defensive and guarded with other people.

Self-worth developed in early childhood and was formed from the interaction of the child with the mother and father. As a child grows older, interactions with significant others will affect feelings of self-worth.

Rogers believed that we need to be regarded positively by others; we need to feel valued, respected, treated with affection and love. Positive regard is to do with how other people evaluate and judge us in social interaction.

Distinction between unconditional positive regard and conditional positive regard

- **Unconditional positive regard:** Unconditional positive regard is where parents, significant others (and the humanist therapist) accepts and loves the person for what he or she is. Positive regard is not withdrawn if the person does something wrong or makes a mistake.

  The consequences of unconditional positive regard are that the person feels free to try things out and make mistakes, even though this may lead to getting it worse at times. People who are able to self-actualize are more likely to have received unconditional positive regard from others, especially their parents in childhood.
- **Conditional positive** regard is where positive regard, praise, and approval, depend upon the child, for example,

behaving in ways that the parents think correct. Hence the child is not loved for the person he or she is, but on condition that he or she behaves only in ways approved by the parent(s).

CONCLUSION

This unit emphasizes the importance of insight learning of Kohlberg, cognitive development of Bruner, Piaget's intellectual development, learning styles of Kolb and Self-actualization of Maslow. It also explains Carl Roger's theory of a fully functioning person which will speak of self or self-concept, self-worth and ideal-self of human being.

QUESTIONS

1. Explain Kohlberg's stages of moral development with examples.
2. Explain Bruner's theory of concept development and its Educational implication.
3. Describe the Maslow's hierarchy of needs and bring out its educational implication.
4. Discuss the learning style theory of Kolb.
5. Explain the different the stages of intellectual development of Piaget.

5

Theory of Constructivism

INTRODUCTION

The new view of the learning process, based on researches that have emerged from the leading learning theories propounded by Vygotsky, Piaget, Bruner and Ausubel, during the late 20th century, is known as the constructive learning. In this view, learners are active, and the learning process is seen as meaning making in socially, culturally, historically and politically situated contexts.

MEANING

Learning is construction of knowledge, which is based on the idea that learning occurs when a learner actively constructs a knowledge representation in working memory. According to this view; the learner is a sense maker whereas the teacher is a cognitive guide who provides guidance and modeling an authentic task. The instructional designer's role is to create environments in which the learner interacts meaningfully with academic material, including fostering the learner's processes of selecting, organizing and integrating information.

Learning activities in constructivist settings are characterized by active engagement, inquiry, problem solving and collaboration with others rather than a dispenser of knowledge; a teacher is a guide, facilitator and co-explorer, who encourage learners to question, challenge and formulate their own ideas, opinions and conclusions. Correct answers and single interpretations are de-emphasized. While there are commonly accepted attributes of constructivism, there are also different interpretations of it. In general, two broad interpretations can be found among contemporary educators: Psychological constructivism articulated by Piaget; and Social constructivism associated with Vygotsky. Two major issues shape these interpretations: (i) education for social transformation; and (ii) the degree of influence that social context has on individual cognitive development.

DEFINITIONS

According to Cannella & Reiff, 1994, "Constructivism is an epistemology, a learning or meaning-making theory that offers an explanation of the nature of knowledge and how humans learn. It maintains that individuals create or construct their own understandings or knowledge through the interactions and activities with which they have contact".

According to Kroll & Boskey, 1996 "Knowledge is acquired through involvement with content instead of imitation or repetition".

According to Wolffe and McMullen, 1996, "Constructivism is primarily a theory of learning, not a theory of teaching."

NATURE OF CONSTRUCTIVIST LEARNER

Constructivist scholars view learning as an active process where learners should learn to discover principles, concepts and facts for themselves, hence the importance of encouraging guesswork and intuitive thinking in learners. In fact, for the social constructivist, reality is not something that we can discover because it does not pre-exist prior to our social invention of it. Kukla (2000) argues that reality is constructed by our own activities and that people, together as members of a society, invent the properties of the world.

Other constructivist scholars agree with this and emphasize that individuals make meanings through the interactions with each other and with the environment they live in. Knowledge is thus a product of humans and is socially and culturally constructed. McMahon (1997) agrees that learning is a social process. He further states that learning is not a process that only takes place inside our minds, nor is it a passive development of our behaviours that is shaped by external forces and that meaningful learning occurs when individuals are engaged in social activities.

The learning environment should also be designed to support and challenge the learner's thinking. While it is advocated to give the learner ownership of the problem and solution process, it is not the case that any activity or any solution is adequate. The critical goal is to support the learner in becoming an effective thinker. This can be achieved by assuming multiple roles, such as consultant and coach.

The following Nature of Constructivist Learner:

1. Learners construct their own knowledge beginning with what they already know, exploring what needs to be known next and determining the quality and effectiveness of their pursuit through authentic assessment and application.
2. All learning begins in doubt about the validity of an idea. The goal of doubt is the restoration of belief.
3. Learning takes place in the personal zone of cognitive development between what is already known, what is not known and what is desired to be known (Vygotsky).
4. Learning is achieved best through a socially interactive process.
5. Learning is best achieved when the undertaking is consistent with the stages of human development.
6. Learning is an experience based process of inquiring, discovering, exploring, doing and undergoing.
7. The process of coming to know is neither random nor eclectic, it has structure.
8. Learning proceeds in spiraling fashion including laddering, scaffolding, weaving, and dialogism.
9. Cognitive development occurs in a socio-cultural context – the social milieu of individual achievement and the

interaction between the learner and adults as well as his/her peers in culturally valued activities.

10. The interactive process in coming to know needs to be guided by structured cognitive and affective taxonomies.

IMPORTANCE OF CONSTRUCTIVIST LEARNER

Social constructivism - encourages culturalism the learner to arrive at their version of the truth, influenced by his or her background, culture or embedded worldview.

Learner is Responsible

It is argued that the responsibility of learning should reside increasingly with the learner. Social constructivism thus emphasizes the importance of the learner being actively involved in the learning process, unlike previous educational viewpoints where the responsibility is rested with the instructor to teach and where the learner played a passive, receptive role.

High Motivation is must

The most crucial thing regarding the nature of learner is that they should have high motivation for learning. According to Von Glaserfeld (1989), sustained motivation to learn is strongly dependent on the learner's confidence in their potential for learning.

Learner is Active

The student is the person who creates new understanding for themselves. The teacher coaches, moderates, suggest but allow the students to do experiments, ask questions, learning activities require the students' full participations. An important part of the learning process is that students reflect on, and talk about their activities. Students are also helped set their own goals and means of assessment.

Learning is Reflective

Students control their own learning process and they lead the way by reflecting on their experiences. This process makes them experts of their own learning. The teacher helps to create situations where the students feel to ask questioning and reflecting on their own processes.

Collaborative Learning

There are many reasons for collaboration which contributes to learning. The main reason in constructivism is that students learn about learning not only by themselves, but also from their peers. When students review and reflect on their learning they can pick up strategies and methods from one another.

Enquiry based Learning

The main activity in a constructivist classroom is solving problems. Students use inquiry methods to ask questions, investigate a topic, and use a variety of resources to find solutions and answers.

ROLE OF TEACHER IN THE CONSTRUCTIVIST CLASSROOM

Teacher encourages students' initiatives and gives freedom and encouragement.

1. The teacher asks open-ended questions and waits for responses.
2. Teacher emphasizes higher-level thinking and reasoning.
3. Students are engaged in dialogue with the teacher and with each other.
4. Teacher encourages reciprocal learning environment in the classroom.
5. Teacher emphasizes on inquiry-based learning.
6. Teacher emphasis on problem-based learning.
7. Cognitive apprenticeships, various methods involving collaboration or group work, co-operative learning (reciprocal questioning, Jig-saw classroom, and structured controversies) are emphasized.
8. The following are four phases in planning and implementing co-operative learning lessons.
    - Making decisions before the lesson begins,
    - Setting the lesson,
    - Monitoring and interviewing during group work; and
    - Evaluating the product and the process of group work.

Other role of teacher in these phases is highlighted below:

1. Making decision before the lesson begins

The teacher is required to formulate academic and social objectives to be realized by students through the co-operative lesson. Academic objectives refer to content, subject matter and the skills to be learnt. Social objectives refer to the social interaction skills to be acquired by the students.

2. Setting lesson

The teacher explains the academic task to the members of the group. He/she also explains to them that they are to accomplish the academic task and to develop social skills too. The teacher needs to ensure that students comprehend their learning task before they begin.

3. Monitoring and intervening during group work

While the students of working, the teacher needs to move around in the class room with a view to monitoring students progress and to intervene if necessary. If the teacher finds that the student facing difficulty in accomplishing the task, they may intervene to provide them assistance in accomplishing to task and help them to overcome the problem.

4. Evaluating the product and process of group work

The teacher needs to provide opportunities to students to evaluate the accomplishment of the academic task and the development of social skills on the part of the students.

NATURE OF LEARNING PROCESS

Constructivist theory states that knowledge is constructed by the learner in working memory. In this construction process the learner uses both incoming material from the environment and prior knowledge from long term memory. SOI model is a theory of learning that can be used to generate instructional implications.

This is called SOI model to highlight the crucial cognitive processes, S for selecting, O for organizing and I for Integrating.

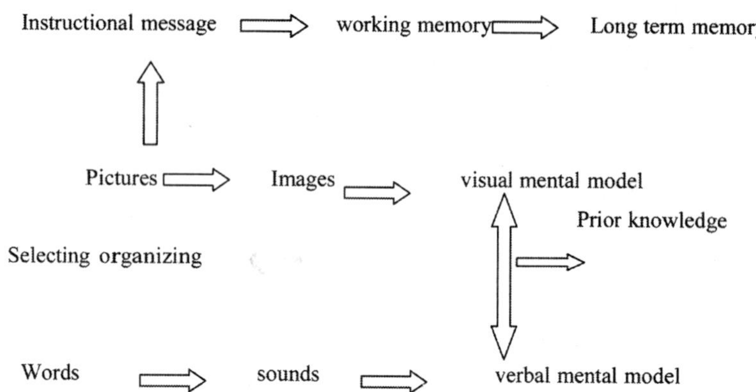

SELECTING RELEVANT INFORMATION

The first process is the selection of relevant information for further processing. When words and pictures are presented to learn in an instructional message, the learner represents them briefly in sensory memories, because of the limited capacity of the human information processing system.

ORGANIZING INCOMING INFORMATION

The selected auditory representation is organized into a coherent verbal representation and the selected images are organized into a coherent pictorial representation. In this process the retained visual images are connected by appropriate links (such as cause and effect); likewise the retained verbal representations are also connected. This activity takes place in working memory. The outcome of this process is the construction of the coherent pictorial representation.

INTEGRATING INCOMING INFORMATION

In this process students make one to one connections between corresponding elements of the pictorial and verbal representations they have constructed using prior knowledge. A final step in learning process is encoding in which the mental representations constructed in working memory are stored in long-term memory for permanent retention.

COLLABORATION AMONG LEARNERS

1. There is a positive interdependence among members of a group.
2. Collaborative learning groups share common goal. They work collaborative to realize the goal.
3. A collaborative learning group does not select its group leader. Rather leadership is shared among its members.
4. The progress of the group as well of each individual is monitored and assessed. As a consequence, an individual is accountable to himself/herself and the group too.
5. In collaborative learning groups, students not only accomplish the academic task but also develop and practice social skills.
6. The teacher and/or the students evaluate the functioning of their group and formulate a plan to improve its functioning in the next collaborative lesson session.
7. In collaborative learning sessions, students help and encourage each other with a view to ensuring that all the members of the collaborative group accomplish the assigned task.
8. Students are required to maintain effective working relationship among them in the group. In the absence of such a relationship, the desired task may not be achieved.
9. Seating arrangement of the members of a group is so made that facilitates interaction among its numbers. The interaction contributes significantly to the realization of the goal of the group.

PEDAGOGICAL APPROACHES TO CONSTRUCTIVISM

Learning involves combining what we know with what was taught, or continually connecting prior knowledge with new information. This prior knowledge can facilitate, inhibit or transform learning. Research on the nature of children's science, (the ideas and experiences students bring into class with them), shows that the students hold their prior ideas tenaciously. These alternative conceptions or misconceptions grow out of students' prior experiences with the world around them and often interface considerably with teachers' attempts to foster learning. Teachers need to analyse students' prior knowledge, connect to it and allow students to build from and onto their prior knowledge. In order to make use of ideas taught by teachers for the students, in the way teachers intend knowledge must present itself as intelligible, fruitful and plausible. This is a move away from a discovery approach, where students construct knowledge solely based on their own experience to knowledge construction where students have the opportunity to test their knowledge within a social context.

The social aspect of knowledge provides clear implications for practice. Learning is seen to be an active process of knowledge construction and sense making. Beyond that, knowledge is understood as a cultural artifact of people. It is created and transformed by each individual and by groups of people. Participating in community discourse allows students to clarify, defend, elaborate, evaluate and argue over the knowledge constructed. Many teachers use cooperative learning as a route to building community discourse in their classrooms. The broader knowledge base for teaching, which included content knowledge, pedagogical content knowledge (PCK), curriculum knowledge, general pedagogy, learners and their characteristics, educational contexts and educational purposes involves the transformation of content knowledge by teachers in different ways that allow the learners to construct knowledge during classroom practice.

Teachers derive PCK from their understandings of content, their own teaching practice and their own schooling experience. As such PCK is closely intertwined with both content knowledge and pedagogical process knowledge. Research in pedagogical content knowledge reinforces the research in cognitive science. Teacher education programmers can enhance the development of PCK in student teachers by modeling and sharing teaching decisions and strategies with students. Faculty should have opportunities to demonstrate and reflect on how they use PCK in their own teaching.

Although it is difficult to separate PCK from content knowledge, a thorough and coherent understanding of content is necessary for effective PCK. Teacher education programmes can assist pre-service teachers in constructing a deep understanding of disciplinary content from a teaching perspective. A teacher education programme which balances attention to the process of learning with the content being learned can ultimately result in helping teachers be able to understand better both their content and the learning of their students. Often content is taught without any attention to process, or process is taught without a deep understanding of the content involved.

GAGNE HIERARCHY OF LEARNING

Robert Gagne was an American educational psychologist, best known for his conditions of learning. His focus was on intentional or purposeful learning, which is a type of learning that occurs in school or specific training programmes. He believed that events in the environment influence the learning process. The theory identifies the general type of human capabilities that are learned, in terms of behavioral changes, once the learning outcomes are identified, an analysis of conditions of learning is done.

Gagne identified eight basic types and arranged them in the hierarchical order. According to Gagne, the higher orders of learning in the hierarchy build upon the lower levels, requiring progressively to greater amount of previous orders for their success. The lowest four orders tend to focus on the behavioral learning and highest four on cognitive learning sample tasks function as real components of a more complex task. The underlying assumption of the hierarchy is that the basic skills are necessary to perform the most complex skill (problem solving).

Signal Learning - This is the simplest form of learning and consist Pavlov's classical conditioning response, where the individual learns to carry out a general conditioned response towards a given signal. The subject is conditioned to emit a desired response as a result of stimulus.

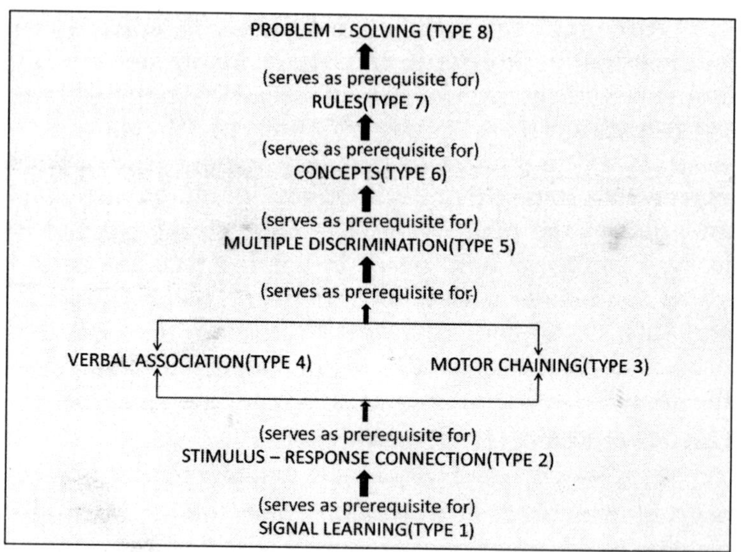

Stimulus Response Learning - This form of learning is also known as Skinner's operant conditioning. The individual shows a certain Response (R) to a discriminated stimulus (S).

Psychomotor Connection learning/chaining - This is a more advanced form of learning in which the subject develops the ability to connect two or more previously-learned stimulus response bonds into a linked sequence.

Verbal Association Learning - It is a form of chaining in which the links between the items being connected are verbal in nature. Verbal association is one of the important processes in the development of language skills.

Multiple Discrimination Learning - Separate associations which have been learnt are connected to form multiple discrimination. This involves developing the ability to make appropriate (different) responses to a series of similar stimuli that differ in a systematic way.

Concept Learning - It is the learning to respond to a stimulus according to abstract characteristics such as position, shape, colour and not according to the concrete physical characteristics.

Principle Learning - A principle is a chain of two or more concepts. In principle learning, one needs to associate more than one concept.

Problem solving - This is the highest level of cognitive process according to Gagne. It involves developing the ability to invent a complex rule, algorithm for the purpose of solving the problem.

Educational Implications:

1. Helping the learner recall what he has previously learned.
2. Determining the sequences of learning.
3. It helps the teacher select appropriate teaching technique.
4. It helps the teacher to break a complete task into component skills and teach those skills only that the students are lacking.
5. It helps the teacher select appropriate test-items for assessing each learning behaviour.

CONCLUSION

Teacher education provides a multiplier effect. As the model that leads our students to understand content deeply and to view content and process as inseparable aspects of knowledge construction approaches, our students gain the perspectives and abilities to move their students to deeper understandings of content. Powerful teacher education should help students at all levels of schooling for better appreciations of the world around them. A constructivist approach shows that content and process are not dichotomous. As more teachers come to that understanding, many more students will benefit.

QUESTIONS

1. Explain constructive approach to learning.
2. Explain the characteristics of constructive approach.
3. Write about the educational implications of constructive approach to learning
4. How does learning take place in constructive approach?

6

Learner – Centered Teaching

INTRODUCTION

Student-centered learning, also known as learner-centered education, broadly encompasses methods of teaching that shift the focus of instruction from the teacher to the student. In original usage, student-centered learning aims to develop learner autonomy and independence by putting responsibility for the learning path in the hands of students. Student-centered instruction focuses on skills and practices that enable lifelong learning and independent problem-solving. Student-centered learning theory and practice are based on the constructivist learning theory that emphasizes the learner's critical role in constructing meaning from new information and prior experience.

MEANING

Learner-centered teaching is an approach to teaching that is increasingly being encouraged in higher education. Learner-centered teachings do not employ a single teaching method. This approach emphasizes a variety of different types of methods that shift the role of the instructors from givers of information to facilitating student learning. Traditionally, instructors focused on what they did, and not on what the students learnt. Educators call this traditional method, "instructor-centered teaching." In contrast, "learner-centered teaching" occurs when instructors focus on student learning.

LEARNER-CENTERED TEACHING/LEARNER - CENTERED LEARNING

Educators commonly use three phrases with this approach. Learner-centered teaching places the emphasis on the person who is doing the learning (Weimer, 2002). Learning-centered teaching focuses on the process of learning. Both phrases appeal to faculty because these phrases identify their critical role of teaching in the learning process. The phrase student centered learning is also used, but some instructors do not like it because it appears to have a consumer focus, seems to encourage students to be more empowered, and appears to take the teacher out of the critical role.

Learner-centered teaching methods shift the focus of activity from the teacher to the learners. These methods include active learning, in which students solve problems, answer questions, formulate questions of their own, discuss, explain, debate, or brainstorm during class; cooperative learning, in which students work in teams on problems and projects under conditions that assure both positive interdependence and individual accountability; and inductive teaching and learning, in which students are first presented with challenges (questions or problems) and learn the course material in the context of addressing the challenges. Inductive methods include inquiry-based learning, case-based instruction, problem-based learning, project-based learning, discovery learning, and just-in-time teaching. Student-centered methods have repeatedly been shown to be superior to the traditional teacher-centered approach to instruction, a conclusion that applies whether the assessed outcome is short-term mastery, long-term retention, or depth of understanding of course material, acquisition of critical thinking or creative problem-solving skills, formation of positive attitudes toward the subject being taught, or level of confidence in knowledge or skills.

DEFINITIONS

"The aim of education should be to teach us rather how to think, than what to think—rather to improve our minds, so as to enable us to think for ourselves, than to load the memory with the thoughts of other men." *- John Dewey*

"The best teacher is the one who suggests rather than dogmatizes, and inspires his listener with the wish to teach himself." *- Edward G. Bulwer-Lytton*

"Do not train a child to learn by force or harshness; but direct them to it by what amuses their minds, so that you may be better able to discover with accuracy the peculiar bent of the genius of each." *- Plato*

"There is nothing as useless as doing efficiently that which should not be done at all." *- Peter Drucker*

FIVE CHARACTERISTICS OF LEARNER CENTERED TEACHING

Active learning, student engagement and other strategies that involve students and mention learning are called learner-centered. And although learner-centered teaching and efforts to involve students have a kind of bread and butter relationship, they are not the same thing. In the interest of more definitional precision, I'd like to propose five characteristics of teaching that make it learner-centered.

1. Learner-centered teaching engages students in the hard, messy work of learning

Teachers are doing too many learning tasks for students. We ask the questions, we call on students, and we add detail to their answers. We offer the examples. We organize the content. We do the preview and the review. On any given day, in most classes teachers are working much harder than students. I'm not suggesting we never do these tasks, but I don't think students develop sophisticated learning skills without the chance to practice and in most classrooms the teacher gets far more practice than the students.

2. Learner-centered teaching includes explicit skill instruction

Learner-centered teachers teach students how to think, solve problems, evidence, analyze arguments, generate hypotheses all those learning skills essential to mastering material in the discipline. They do not assume that students pick up these skills on their own, automatically. A few students do, but they tend to be the students most like us and most students aren't that way. Research consistently confirms that learning skills develop faster if they are taught explicitly along with the content.

3. Learner-centered teaching encourages students to reflect on what they are learning and how they are learning it

Learner-centered teachers talk about learning. In casual conversations, they ask students what they are learning. In class they may talk about their own learning. They challenge student assumptions about learning and encourage them to accept responsibility for decisions they make about learning; like how they study for exams, when they do assigned reading, whether they revise their writing or check their answers. Learner-centered teachers include assignment components in which students reflect, analyze and critique what they are learning and how they are learning it. The goal is to make students aware of themselves as learners and to make learning skills something students want to develop.

4. Learner-centered teaching motivates students by giving them some control over learning processes

Teachers make too many of the decisions about learning for students. Teachers decide what students should learn, how they learn it, the pace at which they learn, the conditions under which they learn and then teachers determine whether students have learned. Students aren't in a position to decide what content should be included in the course or which textbook is best, but when teachers make all the decisions, the motivation to learn decreases and learners become dependent. Learner-centered teachers search out ethically responsible ways to share power with students. They might give students some choice about which assignments they complete. They might make classroom policies something students can discuss. They might let students set assignment deadlines within a given time window. They might ask students to help create assessment criteria.

5. Learner-centered teaching encourages collaboration

It sees classrooms (online or face-to-face) as communities of learners. Learner-centered teachers recognize, and research consistently confirms, that students can learn from and with each other. Certainly the teacher has the expertise and an obligation to share it, but teachers can learn from students as well. Learner-centered teachers work to develop structures that promote shared commitments to learning. They see learning individually and collectively as the most important goal of any educational experience.

Characteristics of Learner-Centered Learning

1. Learning goals are explicitly articulated, students receive feedback on their progress towards meeting those goals, assessments are aligned with those goals, and results of assessment are used iteratively to improve the course.
2. Faculty is aware of common misconceptions in their fields and design opportunities to explicitly engage those during class time. Research has shown that misconceptions can be difficult to cognitively rewire unless students directly encounter the misinformation and build a new understanding.
3. Faculty ascertains what students already know and explicitly integrate new information into that knowledge. Connections between what is being learned and what is known must be made at a neurological level in order for material to be understood and remembered. This theory is called constructivism in the learning literature.
4. Students receive frequent (daily), directed, and timely feedback. The feedback should allow students to correct their understandings and improve their performances

in real time. This practice with feedback is distinct from performance on an exam. 'Feedback' does not necessarily mean a graded assignment. Other modes of feedback include: conversation with peers; labeling a blank diagram followed by viewing of a completed diagram; briefly responding to a question followed by projection of an answer and then self-assessment, and the use of 'clicker' strategies.

5. Student learning is assessed at multiple levels (knowledge, application, analysis, evaluation, generating hypotheses) using multiple formats (multiple choice, essays, solving open-ended problems, project completion, laboratory, oral examination). Assessments are consistent with learning goals. For instance, if interpretation of experimental data is a goal, students need to be assessed on this.
6. Material is presented in several formats (verbal, pictorial, simulation, animation, quantitative) and/or students are asked to do multiple things with the information (listen, write, label, discuss, interpret, graph, hypothesize). Care must be taken not to overdo this approach. Evidence also exists that students can experience cognitive overload (too much information to process it all) and/or be distracted by features that are tangential.
7. Students are encouraged to explain material to themselves and others. Opportunities to elaborate on answers are also provided. For instance, faculty might ask students to explain the logic behind an answer or elaborate on their reasoning.
8. Faculty create an environment in which student understand that performance is linked to effort rather than inherent ability. Intelligence is malleable and academic success can be achieved with hard work and persistence, even when students have gaps in their preparation.
9. Students regularly engage in communication and collaboration with peers. Not only has such

communication been shown to improve learning, it also contributes to the building of a community of learners in the classroom, which is a hallmark of learning-friendly environment.

NEED FOR LEARNER CENTERED APPROACH

Strong, research evidence exists to support the implementation of learner-centered approaches instead of instructor-centered approaches. Knowledge of this research helps instructors defend their teaching methods to their students and to more traditional faculty peers. A task force of the American Psychological Association integrated this research into fourteen Learner-Centered Psychological Principles which can be summarized through the following five domains.

1. **The knowledge base.** The conclusive result of decades of research on knowledge base is that what a person already knows largely determines what new information he attends to, how he organizes and represents new information, and how he filters new experiences, and even what he determines to be important or relevant.
2. **Strategic processing and executive control.** The ability to reflect on and regulate one's thoughts and behaviors is an essential aspect of learning. Successful students are actively involved in their own learning, monitor their thinking, think about their learning, and assume responsibility for their own learning.
3. **Motivation and affect.** The benefits of learner-centered education include increased motivation for learning and greater satisfaction with school; both of these outcomes lead to greater achievement. Research shows that personal involvement, intrinsic motivation, personal commitment, confidence in one's abilities to succeed, and a perception of control over learning lead to more learning and higher achievement in school.
4. **Development and individual differences.** Individuals progress through various common.

5. Stages of development, influenced by both inherited and environmental factors. Depending on the context or task, changes in how people think, believe, or behave are dependent on a combination of one's inherited abilities, stages of development, individual differences, capabilities, experiences, and environmental conditions.
6. **Situation or context.** Theories of learning that highlight the roles of active engagement and social interaction in the students' own construction of knowledge strongly supports this learner-centered paradigm. Learning is a social process. Many environmental factors including how the instructor teaches, and how actively engaged the student is in the learning process positively or negatively influence how much and what students learn (Lambert & McCombs, 2000). In comparison studies between students in lecture and active learning courses, there are significantly more learning gains in the active learning courses.

Advantages of Learner Centered Teaching

- It improves learning achievement of students.
- It leads to better retention of the learnt material.
- It improves self – esteem of students.
- It facilitates interaction among group members and stimulates their thinking process to find solution to the problems which they encounter in accomplishing the assigned task.
- It fosters students reasoning power.

Learner Centered Approaches in teaching:

(i) Individual learning
(ii) Self Learning
(iii) Peer-Group Learning
(iv) Small Group- learning
(v) Whole class learning

1. Individual learning

Individual Learning is a process for setting goals, making a plan to achieve them, and evaluating your progress. Psychology has pointed out that individuals differ in their intelligence, aptitudes, motivation, interest, abilities growth and development; as such it is futile to offer same kind of education to all. It is utmost important to cater to individual differences, if education is to be effective and helpful for optimum development of every individual; otherwise there is every danger of human resources being wasted, resulting in the set back of the society. It is also not practically possible to appoint a tutor for every individual learner.

Steps in individual instruction:

Teachers attempting to provide for individualized instructional packages" should employ the following steps:

- Mentioning the attainment of the skills after successfully finishing each part of the lesson or content of learning.
- Expressing the learning outcomes (in terms of the cognitive, affective and psycho-motor components) as behavioural objectives for each part of the content of learning.
- By arranging the behavioural objectives sequentially, the content to be learned could be set accordingly as a series of short learning steps or frames.
- Test items to assess the objectives that should have been attained after successfully completing the whole lesson, are to be prepared for the terminal testing(post-test).
- As training for answering the post-test items a small testing item should be included in every learning frame of the text of the individualized package.
- Every frame should contain only a small bit of information so that the learner will be able to answer correctly the test item that follows the frame.
- After finishing each frame of learning, the learner should be provided with the feedback about the correctness of his response to the test item in the frame.

2. Self learning

The process of learning in which the learner assumes primary responsibility for planning, implementing, and evaluating a learning project. The learner chooses what to learn and how to learn, and also decides when to continue and when to end the learning project. Students learn themselves independently without the assistance of a teacher by operating on the instructional material, is called 'self-learning'.

Steps in self learning instruction:

- Take into account the individual differences among the learners.
- Freedom for students to learn (choosing what to learn and self-learn the chosen thing at his own convenient time).
- Allow the learners to proceed at their own speed.
- Ensure mastery learning for each learner.
- Present new ideas based on learner's previous knowledge.
- Provide feedback for each response of the learner.
- Ensure the active participation of each individual learner.

3. Peer-group Learning

A peer group is a social group consisting of humans. Peer groups are an informal primary group of people who share a similar or equal status and who are usually of roughly the same age, Members of a particular peer group often have similar interests and backgrounds, bonded by the premise of sameness.

Principle of peer group learning:

- Values and behaviors are influenced by a peer group.
- Active learning and involvement.
- Enable students to learn through sharing of ideas.
- Entire group must experience positive interdependence, face to face interaction.

- Interaction with other students helps students to assume leadership roles.
- It helps students to discuss & clarify.
- It makes students responsible.
- It helps in team building spirit and more supportive relationships.
- Greater communication skills & self esteem.
- Peer learning can improve the overall quality of student learning.
- Group work may reduce the workload involved in assessing, grading and providing feedback to students.

4. Small Group Learning

Small group is one in which the group is able to accomplish its purpose or to establish a basis either for ongoing discussion or for further contact and collaboration among its members.

Principle of small group learning:

- All members of the group have a chance to speak, expressing their own ideas and feelings freely, and to purpose and finish out their thoughts.
- More ideas can be generated.
- Greater diversity of ideas and opinions.
- More people available to get a task completed.
- Solve the problem
- Resolve a conflict
- Great opportunity for sharing skills and knowledge.

5. Whole class learning

A positive atmosphere can make a classroom a more pleasant place to be and, in turn, a more effective, motivating place to learn. Creating a positive learning environment in your classroom will allow your students to feel comfortable, safe and engaged something that all students deserve. In a classroom where vales and roles remain constant and focus is places on the positive aspects of learning, students will be more open to actively participating in class.

Principle of whole class learning:

- Empower decision making at all levels
- Connect schools with communities
- A focus on student achievement
- Quality teaching is responsive to student learning processes.
- Curriculum goals are effectively aligned.
- Teachers and students engage constructively in goal oriented assessment.
- Learning opportunities are effective and sufficient.
- Multiple tasks and contexts support learning cycles.

ADVANTAGES OF LEARNER CENTERED TEACHING Vs TEACHER CENTERED LEARNING

Teacher - Centered Learning

In Teacher- Centered Learning, students put all of their focus on the teacher. The teacher talks, while the students exclusively listen. During activities, students work alone, and collaboration is discouraged.

Advantages:

- Learning takes place in the classroom.
- The teacher directs all classroom activities; they don't have to worry that students will miss an important topic.
- When education is teacher-centered, the classroom remains orderly. Students are quiet, and the teacher retains full control of the classroom and its activities.
- Teaching and assessing are separate.
- The instructor's role is to be primary information giver and primary evaluator.
- Assessment is used to monitor learning.
- Emphasis is on the right answers.
- Desired learning is assessed indirectly through the use of objectivity score tests.
- Memorization of information.
- Focuses on procedure.

Disadvantages:

- When students work alone, they don't learn to collaborate with other students, and communication skills may suffer.
- Teacher-centered instruction can get boring for students. Their minds may wander, and they may miss important facts.
- Teacher-centered instruction doesn't allow students to express themselves, ask questions and direct their own learning.

LEARNER CENTERED TEACHING

When a classroom operates with student-centered instruction, students and instructors share the focus. Instead of listening to the teacher exclusively, students and teachers interact equally. Group work is encouraged, and students learn to collaborate and communicate with one another. Students learn important communicative and collaborative skills through group work.

Advantages:

- Students learn to direct their own learning, ask questions and complete tasks independently.
- Students are more interested in learning activities when they can interact with one another and participate actively.
- Teaching and assessing are intertwined.
- The instructor's role is to coach and facilitate. The instructor and the students evaluate learning together.
- Assessment is used to promote and diagnose learning.
- Emphasis is on generating better questions and learning from errors.
- Desired learning is assessed directly through papers, projects, performances, portfolios, and the like.
- Instructors and students learn together.
- Students are actively involved in the learning process.

- The teacher creates learning environments and motivated students to accept responsibility for learning.
- Students generate ideas.
- Experiential knowledge.
- Learning extends beyond the classroom; students are able to relate problems and strategies to their lives.
- The function of the content learner- centered teaching include building a strong knowledge foundation and to develop learning skills and learner self awareness.

Disadvantages:

- Because students are talking, classrooms are often busy, noisy and chaotic.
- Teachers must attempt to manage all students'activities at once, which can be difficult when students are working on different stages of the same project.
- Because the teacher doesn't deliver instruction to all students at once, some students may miss important facts.
- Some students prefer to work alone, so group work can become problematic.

LEARNER CENTERED TECHNIQUES OF TEACHING AND THEIR ADVANTAGES

Learner-centered teaching or student-centered learning. Educators commonly use three phrases with this approach. Learner- centered teaching places the emphasis on the person who is doing the learning (Weimer, 2002). Learning-centered teaching focuses on the process of learning. Both phrases appeal to faculty because these phrases identify their critical role of teaching in the learning process. The phrase student centered learning is also used, but some instructors do not like it because it appears to have a consumer focus, seems to encourage students to be more empowered, and appears to take the teacher out of the critical role.

Learner centered teaching Vs. Teacher centered learning

Teacher-centered Learning	Learner-centered Teaching
1. Knowledge is transmitted from professor to students.	1. Students construct knowledge through gathering and synthesizing information and integrating it with the general skills of inquiry, communication, critical thinking, problem solving and so on.
2. Students passively receive information.	2. Students are actively involved.
3. Emphasis is on acquisition of knowledge outside the context in which it will be used.	3. Emphasis is on using and communicating knowledge effectively to address enduring and emerging issues and problems in real-life contexts.
4. Professor's role is to be primary information giver and primary evaluation.	4. Professor's role is to coach and facilitate Professor and students evaluate learning together.
5. Teaching and assessing are separate.	5. Teaching and assessing are intertwined.
6. Assessment is used to monitor learning.	6. Assessment is used to promote anddiagnose learning.
7. Emphasis is on right answers.	7. Emphasis is on generating better questions and learning from errors.
8. Desired learning is assessed indirectlythrough the use of objectively scored tests.	8. Desired learning is assessed directlythrough papers, projects, performances,portfolios and the like.
9. Focus is on single discipline.	9. Approach is compatible with interdisciplinary investigation.
10. Culture is competitive and individualistic.	10. Culture is co-operative, collaborative and supportive.
11. Only students are viewed as learners.	11. Professors and students learn together.
12. Focus is on instructor.	12. Focus is on both students and instructor.

(Contd...)

Teacher-centered learning	Learner-centered teaching
13. Focus is on language forms and structures (what the instructor knows about the language).	13. Focus is on language use in typical situations (how students will use the language).
14. Students work alone.	14. Students work in pairs, in groups or alone depending on the purpose of activity.
15. Instructor monitors and corrects every students utterance.	15. Students talk without constant instructor monitoring; instructor provides feedback correction when question arise.
16. Instructor chooses topics.	16. Students have some choice of topics.
17. Instructor evaluates student learning.	17. Students evaluates their own learning, instructor also evaluates.
18. Classroom is quite.	18. Classroom is often noisy and busy.

1. Programmed instruction
2. CAI
3. Self learning
4. Project method
5. Problem solving
6. Field trip

1. Programmed Instruction

An individualized learning techniques called Programmed instruction was introduced in 1950. In this with use of Stimulus –Response-reinforcement cycles individual learners plan to self-learn a whole lesson. For this they may use a specially prepared booklet, teaching machine or computer. In programmed instruction

1. The content of the whole lesson is divided in to a number of small bits of information an one such bit is presented at a time, as a frame.
2. Every frame contains a small bit of information of the content followed by a question (called stimulus) based on the information contained in the frame. After learning a frame, the learner is required to answer the question in the frame (response is elicited).
3. Before proceeding to the next frame, the learner is informed whether his answer is right or wrong (Providing feedback).
4. Frames are arranged sequentially according to this progress of the content of the lesson. Research finding indicate that any student learning through programmed instruction can achieved 90% mastery of Knowledge.

Principles of Programmed Instruction:

1. Principle of small steps
2. Principle of active response
3. Principle of feedback through knowledge of results
4. Principle of self-pacing
5. Principle of student testing or recording of learning.

2. CAI (Computer-Assisted Instruction)

Computer-Assisted Instruction can be used to impart formal and non-formal education at all levels and also in all areas. This CAI has been developed from the principles of programmed instruction. It is one of the types of individualized instruction. In general CAI refers to a system of educational instruction performed almost entirely by computer. The following steps need to be followed.

- Assessing student capabilities with a pre-test
- Presenting educational materials in a navigable form
- Providing repetitive drills to improve the student's command of knowledge
- Providing game-based drills to increase learning enjoyment
- Assessing student progress with a post-test
- routing students through a series of courseware instructional programmed
- Recording student scores and progress for later inspection by a courseware instructor.
- CAI is suitable for all types teaching and learning activities.

Benefits of CAI:

- Self- pacing.
- Re-teaching and reinforcing.
- Personalized feedback of instruction.
- Acquiring knowledge through games.
- Simulations.
- Teaching small increment.
- Immediate feedback
- Are excellent for drill and practice.

Limitations of CAI:

- A poor substitute for actual experience
- Software limitations
- Lack of human qualities

3. Self-Learning

The process of learning in which the learner assumes primary responsibility for planning, implementing and evaluating learning project. The learner chooses what to learn and how to learn and also decide how to continue and when to end the learning project.

Goals of Self-Learning:

- Enhance ability of adults to be more self- directed in learning.
- Foster transformational learning
- Promote social action.

Merits:

- Students become an independent thinker.
- Students learn to accept responsibility.
- Students gain the freedom to learn without restriction.
- Self-learning gives the opportunity to develop a good work ethic.
- Present new ideas based on learner's previous knowledge.
- Allow the learners to proceed at their own speed.

4. Project method

A project is a problematic act carried to completion in the natural setting. In this method the teacher will work as a mere guide for the people and the people will play a important role.

Steps in Project Method:

1. Providing a Situation

The teacher can create a situation in such a way the pupils can frame themselves the problems which are interesting to them to work as a group.

2. Choosing and Proposing the Topic

Based on the situation the pupils should choose or propose a topic. The teacher should give a final touch to that proposal through suggestions. The teacher should also see whether this is suitable to all the pupils or not and also should verify.

3. Planning

The success of the project lies mainly on the good planning under the supervision of the teacher. The teacher should motivate the pupil to participate freely and actively in the discussion. This helps the pupil for a good design of a plan for their proposed project.

4. Executing

A pupil's duty list has to be prepared for the entire work based on their abilities and interest. The teacher should be in the background and should have a proper control over the entire work.

5. Evaluation of the Project

After the entire work of the project is over the pupil should list down the various short comings and difficulties they faced while finishing the project also it is the duty of the teacher to verify whether the objectives of the project have been fulfilled or not.

6. Recording of the Entire Work

A record of the work, their planning, discussion on significant aspects, their achievement,etc., has to be developed by the pupils at the end. Also they should record the criticism of their own work and the suggestions for further work.

Merits:

- It promotes self confidence among pupils.
- This method provides the pupils a training in critical thinking
- Dignity of labor is developed.
- It is psychologically sound.

Demerits:

- It is not suitable for all topics.
- Only expert teacher can be successful in using this method.
- The whole syllabus cannot be included in the forms of project.

5. Problem Solving

It is a method in which a specific problem is given to the students and they are required to find out the solution through objective reasoning and thinking. Here the teacher acts as a guide and will be in the background of the learners. The students should take active part in finding out the solution to the problem.

Steps in Problem-Solving Method:

1. Recognizing the Problem

The teacher should organize a discussion of the problem and based on the discussion, the teacher should create a problem in such a way that the students should feel that it is their own problem and they should solve it.

2. Defining and Interpreting the Problem

The teacher should explain the problem given to the students in detail or may be interpreted by the students themselves through discussion.

3. Collection of Data related to the problem

The teacher should suggest the available resources like books, journals, periodicals etc with respect to the problem given to the students.

4. Organizing and Evaluating the Data of the Problem

The data collected must be well organized by the students. The teacher can help the students in arranging and classifying the materials collected in a scientific way.

5. Arriving at Final Conclusion

After analyzing all the important points with respect to the problem, a tentative solution may be discussed among the students and finally they will arrive at a conclusion collectively.

6. Verification of the Result

Finally the solution to the problem must be verified by applying this result in new situations to detect the discrepancies if any, in the facts already discovered.

Merits:

- The students will get training in the art of solving a problem in actual life situations.
- Reflective thinking and the power of reasoning can be developed with this method.
- Self-confidence among the students can be developed through this method.

Demerits:

- It is a time consuming process.
- This method is used only for the students studying higher classes.
- All the lessons or topics cannot be taught by this method.

6. Field Trip

Field trip may be defined as "an educational procedure by which the student studies firsthand objects and materials in the natural environment.

Advantages:

- It provides accurate information objects, process and system in their real life setting.
- It provides meaningful direct experience.
- The students learning can be easily diverted towards effective learning.
- Field trips can effectively supplement the classroom learning.

Disadvantages:

- There can be expensive and out of reach for many poor students
- A field trip may be occasional activity which at best supplements some learning segments of the syllabus.

CONCLUSION

Technology is increasingly used in language learning either as a complement to teacher mediated instruction or as the sole means of learning. Although access to technology may present challenges to adult education programs and practitioners, these can be overcome. Online platforms have progressed considerably in recent years and promise to offer increasingly useful, affordable, and accessible application and accessible application and tools for learning. Teachers using technology need to continue to provide opportunities for in-person interaction to promote language and literacy development. Further research is needed on the impact of different used of technology and on uses that promote English acquisition over time. Given the rapid rate of innovations in software and internet access, long –term research studies are needed to understand more about the role and impact of using technology with learning.

QUESTIONS

1. Give the meaning of learner – centered teaching.
2. Explain the characteristics of learner – centered teaching.
3. Write about the need for learner – centered approaches.
4. Explain learner – centered teaching Vs Teacher – centered learning.

7

Teaching in Diverse Classrooms

INTRODUCTION

Diverse teaching in a diverse classroom is a buzz word echoing in the recent scenario of education because diversity means understanding and appreciating interdependence of humanity, cultures and the natural environment. In this regard, planning the course with the multicultural classroom in mind by considering syllabi, course assignments, examples, stories and potential classroom dynamics for the diverse students is important. Likewise the role of the teachers is very significant to handle diverse students. The teachers should have adequate professional knowledge, skills and dispositions to have an impact on diverse learners in diverse settings. We will have extensive ideas about strategies for diverse learners, technique of teaching in diverse classroom and preparation of teachers of diverse classroom are further discussed below.

MEANING, DEFINITIONS AND CONCEPT OF DIVERSE CLASSROOM

The concept of diversity encompasses acceptance and respect. It means understanding that each individual is unique and recognizing our individual differences. These can be along the dimensions of race, ethnicity, gender, sexual orientation, socio-economic status, age, physical abilities, religious beliefs, or other ideologies. It is the exploration of these differences in a safe, positive and nurturing environment. It is about understanding each other and moving beyond simple tolerance to embracing and celebrating the rich dimensions of diversity contained within each individual.

Diversity is a reality created by individuals and groups from a broad spectrum of demographic and philosophical differences. It is extremely important to support and protect diversity because by valuing individuals and groups free from prejudice and by fostering a climate where equity and mutual respect are intrinsic.

"Diversity" means more than just acknowledging and/or tolerating difference. Diversity is a set of conscious practices that involve:

- Understanding and appreciating interdependence of humanity, cultures and the natural environment.
- Practicing mutual respect for qualities and experiences that are different from our own.
- Understanding that diversity includes not only ways of being but also ways of knowing.
- Recognizing that personal, cultural and institutionalized discrimination creates and sustains privileges for some while creating and sustaining disadvantages for others.
- Building alliances across differences so that we can work together to eradicate all forms of discrimination.

Diversity includes, therefore, knowing how to relate to those qualities and conditions that are different from our own and outside the groups to which we belong, yet are present in other individuals and groups. These include but are not limited to age, ethnicity, class, gender, physical abilities and qualities, race, sexual orientation, as well as religious status, gender expression, educational background, geographical location, income, marital status, parental status and work experiences. Finally, we acknowledge that categories of difference are not always fixed but also can be fluid, we respect individual rights to self-identification and we recognize that no one culture is intrinsically superior to another.

TEACHING IN A DIVERSE CLASSROOM

Each year teachers are faced with the daunting task of teaching to a classroom of 20-30 individual students, each with their own learning styles, interests, and abilities. Providing optimal learning for such a diverse group can seem overwhelming. But, there is a simple approach that can be used which will enable all students to succeed, and that approach is simply using variety and choice. Not only does this approach address the multiple learning styles of students, but it also aids in making them independent learners.

While the classroom still needs to have structure (routines, rules, procedures), providing variety within that structured environment can aid in providing optimal learning for all students. Using a variety of instructional approaches such as lectures, PowerPoint presentations, inquiry-based instruction, hands-on experiments, project/problem-based learning, or computer aided instruction, not only addresses the various learning styles of the students in the classroom, but it can help learners become more flexible in their learning.

Most learners do have a preferred learning style; however this does not mean they are strictly dependent on that style to learn. They are also comfortable with and able to learn from several other styles as well. Exposing students to a wide variety of learning styles will enable them to become more flexible learners. It is also beneficial to vary the input devices used and the resources made available in the classroom.

Children have a wide variety of preferred learning devices, therefore making as many available as possible provides for this diversity. For example, when presenting information use audio (songs, speeches, interviews, etc.), video, books, posters, hands-on manipulative, food, and smells. Technology has made available a wide range of resources, such as PowerPoint presentations, live video feeds, chats, and communication. PowerPoint presentations are a great way to present information using a mixture of audio, video, animations (movement), and text. These presentations can also be made available to the students via the computer for them to review at their own pace. The internet/ computers also offer interactive learning activities that combine movement, visuals, and sounds, such as virtual science experiments. These allow students to conduct experiments never before thought possible due to danger or lack of equipment.

Pre-exposure to material also aids in learning. The more familiar students are with a subject the easier it is for new learning to occur. Therefore, providing students with a variety of pre-exposure materials can better prepare them for new learning units.

Novelty can be used to gain and keep students' attention. People usually only pay attention to things that are of value or things that are personally meaningful. Therefore, relating learning to your students' real life experiences or interests can catch and keep their attention.

When planning your lessons it is beneficial to try to include as many of the senses and/or Gardner's multiple intelligences (verbal-linguistic, logical-mathematical, kinaesthetic, visual-spatial, musical, interpersonal, intrapersonal, and naturalist) as possible. You can do this by using a variety of activities in your plans such as songs, games, experiments, field trips, real world experiences, interviews, guest speakers, physical movement/exercise, small group activities, individual activities, partner activities, cooking/ food/snacks, hands-on experiences, etc. Providing a variety of activities will enable students of all ability levels to succeed.

Not only do students have diverse learning styles but varying bio-cognitive cycles as well. Some students learn best in the morning, some in the afternoon. Therefore, having a flexible classroom schedule can provide for these differences. Also, varying the times and types of assessments can give all students a fair chance of showing their true abilities. When applicable, it is beneficial to give students choice in activities and assessments. This provides students opportunities to showcase their individual talents and can aid in classroom management as well.

If students are constantly dictated to and not given a voice or choice they can grow resentful and "act out". Provide a variety of classroom activities for students to choose from during structured and unstructured times, give those several projects such as posters, PowerPoint presentations, reports, interviews, videos, brochures, etc. to choose from when assessing their knowledge. Giving student choice provides them with a sense of empowerment over their learning and can aid them in deciding what learning styles and assessments work best for them, thus helping them become more responsible for their own learning.

It would be a pretty boring world if all learners were the same. Diversity makes the classroom more interesting and exciting. Teachers should honour and respect the uniqueness of each student by offering variety and choice in their classrooms. Not only will this address the diverse needs of the students, but it will also help them to become independent learners as well.

PREPARATIONS OF TEACHERS IN A DIVERSE CLASSROOM

Teaching and learning are the most central activities of education; they involve the teacher, the learner, the content, the strategies, and the context for instruction. The mission of the Department of Instruction and Learning (DIL) is to provide regional, national, and international leadership in the study and improvement of teaching and learning in diverse educational settings.

The department addresses its mission through three interrelated efforts: research, the preparation of teaching/ practitioner professionals, and service. In carrying out these efforts, the faculty shares the goals to: Generate, disseminate, and apply new knowledge about teaching, learning, and performance in various educational settings.

- Identify the factors and features that contribute to the design and implementation of effective professional preparation programs in education.
- Provide exemplary initial preparation and continuing education programs or teachers/specialists in the traditional major academic content areas and in selected related areas central to the operation of effective schools.
- Provide the opportunities for advanced-level students in selected specialized areas to become highly competent scholar-researchers and scholar-practitioners.
- Contribute to the educational development of school-aged, university, and adult students in the region through a variety of direct instructional programs.
- Enhance that development further by contributing to the design and implementation of exemplary school-based programs through various university-school-community partnerships.

How teachers prepare for a diverse classroom?

- Teachers need to meet the needs of an increasingly diverse population.
- Local schools need to provide information on different cultures such as the African American culture.
- Learning styles need to be discussed and applied in the classroom.
- Teachers need to adapt their teaching techniques to multicultural learners.
- Activities such as exploring different cultures or countries needs to be included to help students understand multicultural differences in the classroom.
- Teachers should be aware of personal beliefs and bias concerning their students.

Techniques of Teaching in a Diverse Classroom:

There are many techniques available to teach in a diverse classroom.

1. Brainstorming

In this, all diverse students will discuss a problem interestingly to arrive a solution.

2. Critical incidents

Here, the students make nonverbal communication to explain about a critical incident that took place in their life.

3. Acting it out

It is also a non verbal communication which is practiced by enacting a play.

4. Mime

In this technique, the students do miming for enacting a small kit.

5. Focus of symposium

This is done to engage the diverse learners based on the consideration of the learners, nature of content and desired outcome.

Here are six types of knowledge we can develop to help Diversified learners to succeed in the classroom.

(a) Learn about culture

Become aware of how the influence of your own culture, language, social interests, goals, cognitions and values could prevent you from learning how you could best teach your students of culturally and linguistically diverse backgrounds.

(b) Learn about students' culture

Understand how your students' cultures affect their perceptions, self-esteem, values, classroom behaviour and learning. Use that understanding to help your students feel welcomed, affirmed, respected and valued.

(c) Understand your students' linguistic traits

Learn how students' patterns of communication and various dialects affect their classroom learning and how second-language learning affects their acquisition of literacy.

(d) Use this knowledge to inform your teaching

Let your knowledge of your students' diverse cultures inform your teaching. This, along with a sincerely caring attitude, increases student participation and engagement.

(e) Use multicultural books and materials to foster cross-cultural understanding

Sensitively use multicultural literature, especially children's literature, to honour students' culture and foster cross-cultural understanding. Be open to a variety of instructional strategies as students' cultures may make certain strategies (such as competitive games or getting students to volunteer information) uncomfortable for them.

(f) Know about your students' home and school relationships

Collaborate with parents and caregivers on children's literacy development and don't rely on preconceived notions of the importance of literacy within your students' families.

DIVERSE TEACHING STRATEGIES FOR DIVERSE LEARNERS

Teaching Strategies

There are many school factors that affect the success of culturally diverse students – the school's atmosphere and overall attitudes toward diversity, involvement of the community, and culturally responsive curriculum, to name a few. Of all of these factors, the personal and academic relationships between teachers and their students may be the most influential. This relationship has been referred to as the "core relationship" of learning – the roles of teachers and students, the subject matter, and their interaction in the classroom.

Certain behaviours and instructional strategies enable teachers to build a stronger teaching/learning relationship with their culturally diverse students. Many of these behaviours and strategies exemplify standard practices of good teaching, and others are specific to working with students from diverse cultures. A number of these behaviours and strategies are listed below.

TEACHER BEHAVIOURS

1. Appreciate and accommodate the similarities and differences among the students' cultures

Effective teachers of culturally diverse students acknowledge both individual and cultural differences enthusiastically and identify these differences in a positive manner. This positive identification creates a basis for the development of effective communication and instructional strategies. Social skills such as respect and cross-cultural understanding can be modelled, taught, prompted, and reinforced by the teacher.

2. Build relationships with students

Interviews with African-American high school students who presented behaviour challenges for staff revealed that they wanted their teachers to discover what their lives were like outside of school and that they wanted an opportunity to partake in the school's reward systems. Developing an understanding of students' lives also enables the teacher to increase the relevance of lessons and make examples more meaningful.

3. Focus on the ways students learn and observe students to identify their task orientations

Once students' orientations are known, the teacher can structure tasks to take them into account. For example, before some students can begin a task, they need time to prepare or attend to details. In this case, the teacher can allow time for students to prepare, provide them with advance organizers, and announce how much time will be given for preparation and when the task will begin. This is a positive way to honour their need for preparation, rituals, or customs.

4. Teach students to match their behaviours to the setting

We all behave differently in different settings. For example, we behave more formally at official ceremonies. Teaching students the differences between their home, school, and community settings can help them switch to appropriate behaviour for each context. For example, a teacher may talk about the differences between conversations with friends in the community and conversations with adults at school and discuss how each behaviour is valued and useful in that setting. While some students adjust their behaviour automatically, others must be taught and provided ample opportunities to practice. Involving families and the community can help students learn to adjust their behaviour in each of the settings in which they interact.

INSTRUCTIONAL STRATEGIES

1. **Use a variety of instructional strategies and learning activities:**
   - Offering variety provides the students with opportunities to learn in ways that are responsive to their own communication styles, cognitive styles, and aptitudes.
   - In addition, the variety helps them develop and strengthen other approaches to learning.
2. **Consider students' cultures and language skills when developing learning objectives and instructional activities:**
   - Facilitate comparable learning opportunities for students with differing characteristics.
   - For example, consider opportunities for students who differ in appearance, race, sex, disability, ethnicity, religion, socioeconomic status, or ability.
3. **Incorporate objectives for affective and personal development:**
   - Provide increased opportunities for high and low achievers to boost their self-esteem, develop positive self-attributes, and enhance their strengths and talents.
   - Such opportunities can enhance students' motivation to learn and achieve.
4. **Communicate expectations:**
   - Let the students know the "classroom rules" about talking, verbal participation in lessons, and moving about the room.

- Tell them how long a task will take to complete or how long it will take to learn a skill or strategy, and when appropriate, give them information on their ability to master a certain skill or complete a task. For example, it may be necessary to encourage students who expect to achieve mastery but are struggling to do so.
- They may need to know that they have the ability to achieve mastery, but must work through the difficulty.

5. **Provide rationales:**
   - Explain the benefits of learning a concept, skill, or task.
   - Ask students to tell you the rationale for learning and explain how the concept or skill applies to their lives at school, home, and work.
6. **Use advance and post organizers**
   - At the beginning of lessons, give the students an overview and tell them the purpose or goal of the activity.
   - If applicable, tell them the order that the lesson will follow and relate it to previous lessons. At the end of the lesson, summarize its main points.
7. **Provide frequent reviews of the content learned:**
   - For example, check with the students to see if they remember the difference between simple and compound sentences.
   - Provide a brief review of the previous lesson before continuing on to a new and related lesson.
8. **Facilitate independence in thinking and action:**
   - There are many ways to facilitate students' independence. For example, when students begin their work without specific instruction from the teacher, they are displaying independence.

- When students ask questions, the teacher can encourage independence by responding in a way that lets the student know how to find the answer for him- or herself.
- When teachers ask students to evaluate their own work or progress, they are facilitating independence, and asking students to perform for the class (e.g., by reciting or role-playing) also promotes independence.

9. Promote student on-task behaviour

- Keeping students on task maintains a high level of intensity of instruction.
- By starting lessons promptly and minimizing transition time between lessons, teachers can help students stay on task. Shifting smoothly (no halts) and efficiently (no wasted effort) from one lesson to another and being business-like about housekeeping tasks such as handing out papers and setting up audiovisual equipment helps to maintain their attention.
- Keeping students actively involved in the lessons – for example, by asking questions that require students to recall information – also helps them to stay focused and increases the intensity of instruction.

10. Monitor students' academic progress during lessons and independent work:

- Check with students during seatwork to see if they need assistance before they have to ask for help.
- Ask if they have any questions about what they are doing and if they understand what they are doing.
- Also make the students aware of the various situations in which a skill or strategy can be used as well as adaptations that will broaden its applicability to additional situations.

11. **Provide frequent feedback:**
    - Feedback at multiple levels is preferred. For example, acknowledging a correct response is a form of brief feedback, while prompting a student who has given an incorrect answer by providing clues or repeating or rephrasing the question is another level.
    - The teacher may also give positive feedback by stating the appropriate aspects of a student's performance.
    - Finally, the teacher may give positive corrective feedback by making students aware of specific aspects of their performance that need work, reviewing concepts and asking questions, making suggestions for improvement, and having the students correct their work.
12. **Require mastery:**
    - Require students to master one task before going on to the next.
    - When tasks are assigned, tell the students the criteria that define mastery and the different ways mastery can be obtained.
    - When mastery is achieved on one aspect or portion of the task, give students corrective feedback to let them know what aspects they have mastered and what aspects still need more work. When the task is complete, let the students know that mastery was reached.

Effective Teaching in a Diverse Classroom:

- Teachers have a clear sense of their own ethnic and cultural identities.
- Teachers communicate high expectations for the success of all students and a belief that all students can succeed.
- Teachers are personally committed to achieving equity for all students and believe that they are capable of making a difference in their students' learning.

- Teachers have developed a bond with their students and cease seeing their students as "the other."
- Schools provide an academically challenging curriculum that includes attention to the development of higher-level cognitive skills.
- Instruction focuses on students' creation of meaning about content in an interactive and collaborative learning environment.
- Teachers help students see learning tasks as meaningful.
- Curricula include the contributions and perspectives of the different ethno cultural groups that compose the society.
- Teachers provide "scaffolding" that links the academically challenging curriculum to the cultural resources that students bring to school.
- Teachers explicitly teach students the culture of the school and seek to maintain students' sense of ethno cultural pride and identity.
- Community members and parents or guardians are encouraged to become involved in students' education and are given a significant voice in making important school decisions related to programs (such as resources and staffing).
- Teachers are involved in political struggles outside the classroom that are aimed at achieving a more just and humane society.

EFFECTIVE TEACHING STRATEGIES

This list provides a quick reference to effective teaching strategies to integrate into your classroom. These teaching methodologies are time tested to help you capture your student's attention and motivate them to learn.

Strategies for Direct Instruction:

- Specify clear lesson objectives
- Teach directly to those objectives
- Make learning as concrete and meaningful as possible

- Provide relevant guided practice
- Provide independent practice
- Provide transfer practice activities

Strategies for Students with Disabilities:

- **Sequence** - Break down the task, step by step prompts.
- **Drill-repetition and practice-review** - Daily testing of skills, repeated practice, daily feedback.
- **Segment** - Break down targeted skill into smaller units and then synthesize the parts into a whole.
- **Direct question and response** - Teacher asks process-related questions and/or content-related questions.
- **Control the difficulty or processing demands of a task** - Task is sequenced from easy to difficult and only necessary hints or probes are provided.
- **Technology** - Use a computer, structured text, flow charts to facilitate presentation, emphasis is on pictorial representations.
- **Group Instruction** - Instruction occurs in a small group, students and/or teacher interact with the group.
- **Supplement teacher and peer involvement** - Use homework, parents, or others to assist in instruction.
- **Strategy clues** - Reminders to use strategies or multi-steps, the teacher verbalizes problem solving or procedures to solve, instruction uses think-aloud models.

DIVERSITY IN THE CLASSROOM

Diversity is a term that can have many different meanings depending on context. This module will not offer a comprehensive definition of the term; instead, this module will highlight two key areas related to diversity:

- Identify how diversity affects the classroom
- Provide practical tips for promoting an inclusive classroom

How Diversity affects the Classroom?

Much discussion about diversity focuses on the following forms of marginalization: race, class, gender, and sexual orientation — and rightfully so, given the importance of these forms of difference. In fact, students come to the university classroom with different backgrounds, sets of experiences, cultural contexts, and world views.

Additionally, issues of diversity play a role in how students and teachers view the importance of the classroom and what should happen there. For example, assumptions about what a typical student should know, the resources they have and their prior knowledge are extremely important.

Students may perceive that they do not "belong" in the classroom setting — a feeling that can lead to decreased participation, feelings of inadequacy, and other distractions. Teachers may make flawed assumptions of students' capabilities or assume a uniform standard of student performance. Teachers may themselves feel out of place based on their own ascriptive traits (i.e. differences based on class, privilege, etc.).

Identifying and thinking through notions of difference and how they affect the classroom allow both students and teachers to see the classroom as an inclusive place.

PRACTICAL TIPS FOR PROMOTING AN INCLUSIVE CLASSROOM

While many discussions concerning diversity focus on talking about the importance of diversity and recognizing difference, it is equally important to move to the next step: incorporating specific tips for addressing differences and how they play out.

One way to form strategies for promoting an inclusive classroom is to use self-reflection and think of potential classroom scenarios and how one might address them. The solutions to such scenarios are ones that each teacher should consider for him- or herself, since there are no immediate right or wrong answers.

LEARNING STYLES IN A DIVERSE CLASSROOM

Eddy (1999) describes a learning style as the way in which we prefer to organize, classify and assimilate information about the environment.

AUDITORY LEARNERS

Auditory learners prefer to receive ideas and information by hearing them. These students may struggle with reading and writing, but excel at memorizing spoken words such as song lyrics. They often benefit from discussion-based classes and the opportunity to give oral presentations.

VISUAL LEARNERS

Visual learners prefer to receive information by seeing it. Typically these students pay much attention to detail. They are less likely to speak in class than their auditory peers, and generally use few words when they do. Outlines, graphs, maps and pictures are useful in helping these students learn.

KINAESTHETIC

Tactile learners tend to learn best via movement and touch. These students are often labelled "hyperactive" because they tend to move around a great deal. Because they like movement, they may take many notes and learn best when allowed to explore and experience their environment.

It is important to note that the various styles are those preferred by learners. If we looked at complete descriptions of each style, we would probably see some of ourselves in each. But we could also probably identify our dominant style. The fact that we learn in many ways is further justification for utilizing variety of teaching approaches is so important.

Understanding learning styles can help one to create more inclusive classrooms where everyone has a chance to succeed. For instance, a student from a culture that teaches children to listen quietly in a classroom (or a visual learner who is uncomfortable with speaking) can be at a disadvantage when a portion of the grade is based on participation in class. Sensitive teachers can allow for group work during class to create smaller, safer environments for these students to speak and for their classroom performance to be evaluated.

STUDENTS' SPECIAL NEEDS

Some students will have unique challenges that make learning in a traditional classroom difficult. Examples include visual or hearing impairments, Attention Deficit Disorder, mobility challenges, chronic illness (such as that brought about by chemotherapy), and learning disabilities.

There are many possible accommodations that help to create a productive learning environment for these students. It may be necessary for a student with a hearing impairment to have an interpreter present, for instance. A student with a chronic illness may need you to be flexible about the due dates for assignments.

Below are suggestions to consider when you work with students with special needs:

- Even though two students may have the same disability, their needs for accommodation may be quite different. Treat each student as an individual.
- Keep in mind that disabilities are not always visible to us. You are not required to assess a student's health; you should accept authorized documentation concerning an individual student's needs.
- Using many modes (written, verbal, video/slide, etc.) to present information is one way to help some learners with special needs learn more effectively.

It is important to remember that you are not responsible for identifying the disability or deciding on the accommodations. The office of Disability Services and Programs (DSP) at USC provide students with a letter authenticating their needs and the students should be able to present this letter to you upon request. DSP will help you identify and make the necessary accommodations.

If the student is not able to provide you with this documentation, you should politely explain that, before you can make the accommodations, the student needs to have registered with DSP. You will then work with DSP to determine the accommodations.

CONCLUSION

This chapter describes a multitude of teaching strategies shown by research to be effective in educating diverse student learners. Diverse student learners include students from racially, ethnically, culturally, and linguistically diverse families and communities of lower socioeconomic status. If educators act on the knowledge research offers, we can realize the educational excellence we desire for all children.

QUESTIONS

1. Define diverse class room and diverse learners.
2. What are the techniques of teaching in a diverse class room?
3. Explain the strategies of diverse teaching for the diverse learners.
4. What is the role of a teacher to teach in a racially diverse classroom?
5. Bring out the learning style in a diverse class room.

8

Learning in and out of School

INTRODUCTION

Learning inside school gives pleasure and enthusiasm to the students. It is a natural way of learning. This learning is linked to students' lives and a variety of different teaching methods are used in school whereas, out of school learning consists of curricular and non-curricular learning experiences for pupils. Out of school experiences are organised with community partners such as museums, sport facilities, charity initiatives and more. So, students should be enlightened the advantages of learning in and out of school in a detailed study.

PURPOSE OF LEARNING IN AND OUT OF CLASSROOM

Learning inside the Classroom

It is a concept of traditional but it adopts the natural way of learning. It's a pleasure to learn inside the school rather than outside learning. For the budding children inside learning helps a lot to learn abundant in naturally. Students learn new and newer things only in school setting with the help of the teachers and with models. School is where we have our first experience of formal learning, and how things go for us here can affect how we learn throughout our lives. When school is exciting and involving, it gives us confidence in ourselves as learners, but when it isn't, we can be turned off and think we can't learn or that learning is boring. To make sure children today and tomorrow have good school experiences to sustain their learning in future, the Campaign works with schools and teachers to develop good practice.

The Classroom

The classroom itself is the locus of regular and sustained interactions among students and teachers around curriculum. If the classroom is at the heart of students 'Opportunities to learn, the quality of teachers' instructional practices are of paramount importance. Inside school, Quality Instructional Practices include linking learning to factors that are important in students' lives are taught. Different method is used to make the learning effective and interesting.

Using formative and summative assessments in a systematic manner provides available information to students and significantly improves learning and achievement. Setting objectives and providing regular feedback (including praise) on student progress.

What is a Learning Environment in Classrooms?

Almost all of us have spent a great deal of time in the classroom, beginning in kindergarten and extending for years beyond. Have you ever noticed what the teacher did to make learning more inviting? Was it colorful posters, clear and consistent rules, and fun and interesting teaching methods? If so, you were lucky to have a teacher who paid close attention to the learning environment, or the physical, psychological and instructional atmosphere.

Why are Learning Environments Important?

The learning environment in the classroom is vital to student success and impacts students in many ways. A negative learning environment or setting that adversely affects student learning in many ways, such as low student achievement, poor behavior, student anxiety, or depression. A positive learning environment or one that allows students to feel comfortable and confident as learners.

- **Positive Learning Environment**

The bright posters, organized spaces and cooperative learning arrangements aren't an accident. The use of space includes how furniture is arranged and organized, how materials are stored and maintained, how clean the classroom is and the overall color and brightness. The children need a clean, bright, organized space to strengthen learning experiences.

- **Psychological environment**

The psychological environment in the classroom is how students feel about their learning. The teacher has specific rules and consequences posted in his/her classroom and clearly explains each to students. Teacher has a calm, patient demeanor and is focused on helping students learn, both intellectually and socially. Teacher maintains a positive control of his/her classroom by being a role model for kind words and actions. Teacher knows that students react negatively when they feel things are unfair, unclear or are worried about getting in trouble. Because teacher is clear and consistent, offers praise and gratitude, and sets a good example, students are confident and comfortable in the classroom.

- **Instructional environment**

The instructional environment is the setting for all teaching. Teacher plans his/her instruction to make sure his/her students are able to comprehend by using different teaching practices, such as lecture, hands-on activities, cooperative learning groups and plenty of small group and individual practice. Instructional environment remains positive and upbeat, with an air of fun and excitement. The students will say teacher makes learning interesting and fun, which means they're engaged and will remember content long-term.

Features of Learning in School

- Learning is linked to students' lives.
- A variety of different teaching methods are used.
- Different learning styles are respected.
- High expectations for all students.
- Formative evaluations are used systematically.
- Teachers set clear objectives, monitor progress and provide feedback.
- Opportunities for classroom participation.

- Diversity and individual differences are respected.
- Social and emotional learning is valued.
- Positive student-teacher and student-student relationships.
- Classroom management strategies are systematic.
- Disciplinary strategies are consistent and non- coercive.

ADVANTAGES OF LEARNING INSIDE THE CLASSROOM

- **More Interaction**

A classroom environment offers students the opportunity to have face-to-face interactions with their peers and instructors. This is an added social benefit as well as an educational aid. Because students see the same peers in class every session, they get a chance to form friendships. In the case of higher learning, pupils can find potential lifelong professional connections. On the educational side, students get a chance to participate in a lecture or class discussion physically. If something is not understood, interrupting to ask for clarification is always an option.

- **Traditional Experience**

In some cases, the classroom environment is the only style of education the students know, and the change of pace online classes offer may prove difficult to adjust to. Students get the opportunity for hands-on, structured learning instead of being presented with the course books, written lectures and self-directed activities distance learning provides. Suddenly straying from the standard learning experience may add unexpected strain academically, making the class material more difficult in the process.

DISADVANTAGES OF LEARNING INSIDE THE CLASSROOM

- **No Flexibility**

A campus-based learning experience means the class schedule is predetermined and not subject to change. Students must shape their personal schedules around school instead of the other way around. If plans unexpectedly change or an emergency comes up, the student cannot adjust the class schedule to turn in the work at a different time. If a scheduling conflict arises between work and school, students are forced to choose between their education and their income.

- **Travel Considerations**

With classroom learning, students must physically attend the courses to get credit for attendance. Those who must travel long distances to get to school must allot enough time to arrive punctually, particularly in instances where inclement weather is involved. A long commute may also mean a hefty gas bill over a long period of time which, when combined with the cost of education, may present an issue to financially challenged students.

- **Lacks Student Focused Learning**

A drawback of traditional training is that it inherently places the most value on standards, curriculum and passing tests as opposed to student-focused learning. Student-focused learning places value on the student and builds the curriculum around the questions young people need answered in order to understand the material. Constructivist learning builds on the knowledge students already have allowing them to form concrete associations to new information, which improves retention. Traditional learning is based on repetition and memorization of facts that students care less about and retain at lower rates after testing.

- **Lacks Emphasis on Critical Thinking**

Traditional classroom training doesn't encourage critical thinking skills, the ability to actively apply information gained through experience and reasoning. Instead, traditional training emphasizes the role of teachers as knowledge dispensers and students as repositories. This style of learning doesn't allow student's deeper levels of understanding required for complex concepts and lifelong learning.

- **Lacks Process Oriented Learning**

Traditional training emphasizes passing tests, whether or not students under testing material. The learning process is thus devalued, and students are not encouraged to understand the methods, techniques and skills required to find answers. Constructivist learning holds the process as important as the results because it stimulates skills important long after schooling.

- **Lacks Emphasis on Larger Concepts or Structures**

  Rather than focusing on larger concepts and considering student context in the learning as constructivist training does, traditional training focuses on basic skills and gradually builds to a whole. While this simplifies learning, it provides little context, which can disconnect learners.

- **Lacks Interactivity**

  Traditional training emphasizes individual student work and projects and is poor preparation for a student's future endeavours, which are likely to include working on teams and collaborating with colleagues. Under this training model, students receive few opportunities to practice group dynamics.

PURPOSE OF LEARNING INSIDE THE CLASSROOM

Benefits of an Expedition

From increased confidence and fitness to global awareness and money management, an expedition brings benefits that will have an impact on the rest of your life.

Completing a World Challenge expedition is an educational travel experience that goes on rewarding students, long after they return home. Challengers achieve more than they thought possible by stretching beyond their comfort zone, and this sense of accomplishment colors their ongoing view of themselves and their place in the world. They have to raise the bar in terms of physical fitness, communication, teamwork and organization, all highly valuable skills they can draw on in their post-expedition lives. Engaging with another culture during the Project phase brings global awareness that can't be gleaned from books. Students return from their expedition with increased energy and enthusiasm and a sense that if they really apply themselves, there's no limit to what they can do.

With our support, students take ownership of destination research and itinerary planning, fundraising ideas and events, budgeting, preparation, fitness and nutrition. At World Challenge, we believe this build-up programme is as important as the expedition itself, in teaching young people important life skills such as the teamwork and money management. Our structured educational programmes, led by experienced staff, teach practical skills and encourage students to take responsibility for themselves and their team.

EMPLOYABILITY AND LIFE SKILLS

- **Team Building**

Teamwork is the key to success on every World Challenge expedition. Knowing your team well and having an awareness of the strengths and weakness of others means that you can accomplish more together.

- **Leadership**

An important part of your expedition is taking responsibility for and leading your team, which you all get the opportunity to do, before and during the expedition. Becoming more comfortable in a leader role has positive implications for your chosen career.

- **Problem-Solving**

The nature of travel in developing countries means that expeditions often don't go exactly according to plan. Problems such as illness, poor accommodation, river crossings, eating difficulties and different expectations all impact on them. Dealing with and surmounting these difficulties is a valuable experience that enhances life skills.

Every expedition offers its share of challenge and adventure; this is why we embark on expeditions, to enable us to push ourselves and learn. Having an understanding and appreciation not only for your own safety, but also for that team mates is a crucial life lesson for students.

PURPOSE OF LEARNING OUTSIDE THE CLASSROOM

Learning beyond the classroom offers a whole host of opportunities you'll struggle to find within confines of your classroom's four walls, I've outlined just a few below.

1. Make learning more engaging

It can be difficult to keep kids on task in the classroom. Especially as the school year draws to an end and the weather is nice outside and all they want to do is run around like mad things. Why not take learning outside and let them do just that? Take maths outside and have children estimate then time how long it would take to run, hop and skip across a field. They can discuss it outdoors and graph it back in the classroom.

2. Make learning relevant

By taking learning beyond the classroom you'll find dozens of opportunities to make learning concepts, real and relevant by putting them into a more realistic context. Many concepts which seem too difficult to get a grasp of in the classroom are a lot easier to understand in the big wide world when they're set in context, and when the children are more engaged and motivated to understand and learn.

3. Nurture creativity and imagination

Taking kids beyond the classroom is like unclipping their wings. Suddenly their minds are free to explore and you can often end up with some very creative results no matter what subject you're teaching them. For example, instead of learning about castles in the classroom are you able to take your children to a real castle ruins and have them act in role? You'll be amazed at how their imaginations run wild – but make sure you know your stuff as they'll have no end of questions to ask you to help fuel their role play.

4. Develop learning through play and experimentation

We all know that children learn more when they're happy and engaged. It's amazing just how much they can learn through playing. You can bet that the kids who did the role play in the castle will remember heaps about what life was like for their characters. Experimenting is also a fantastic way to learn – very young children learn a huge amount about volume and textures by simple things like sand and water play, whilst older children will enjoy becoming nature detectives and learning about manifests and their habitats.

5. Improve attendance

If you're able to build outside play – and visits, into your curriculum and engage and motivate your pupils to learn, you'll inevitably find that they're more motivated to turn up to school.

6. Reduce behaviour problems

Whilst learning beyond the classroom certainly means implementing a whole new set of behaviour management processes, on the whole it can often mean a general improvement in behaviour – yet another consequence of children being happy, engaged and motivated. There are not many children who are likely to act up if the consequence is that the whole class has to go back to learning maths inside...

7. Develop interest in the environment and wider surroundings

Learning outside can give you a great opportunity to teach your pupils about the environment and about your local area. This is an important part of developing them as responsible citizens that can be difficult to convey in the classroom.

8. Expose children to new opportunities

Learning outside the classroom doesn't just have to mean wandering around the school grounds, though this is a great place to start. There is no end of places you can take the pupils that they might not get access to otherwise. Museums, galleries, zoos and farms can be of great interest or somewhere where they can find out how things are made and maybe even have a go themselves can provide learning experiences that won't be forgotten fast.

9. Keep healthy

Even if you're just going to work a few feet from the confines of your classroom, well directed outdoor learning opportunities can offer a great opportunity for fresh air and exercise. Even pupils who aren't much interested in Physical Education can usually be tempted by a fun learning game without the pressure of needing to 'win'.

10. Enjoy almost limitless resources

One of the key benefits of learning outside is that you have the most amazingly well resourced stock cupboard you could hope for – and a lot of it is free. No matter how tight your school's budget, so long as you have a good imagination you'll be able to develop free, meaningful learning opportunities for your children that will stick with them.

OBSERVATIONAL LEARNING

Observation Learning is learning that occurs through observing the behaviour of others. It is a form of social learning which takes various forms, based on various processes. In humans, this form of learning seems to not need reinforcement to occur, but instead, requires a social model such as a parent, sibling, friend or teacher. Particularly in childhood, a model is someone of authority or higher status.

This type of learning involves the observation of a response or a sequence of responses on the part of somebody else; and later incorporation and display of these in one's own behaviour. The essential difference between imitational learning and observational learning is that in the former we attempt to repeat the response in to but in the latter we incorporate the observed response in our behaviour pattern and express it as our unique response. For example though we learn walking, writing, dressing, etc. through observation, we form our own style in all these things. Most of our social learning is through observation when we interact in the society in which we live and operate.

According to Bandura's social cognitive learning theory, observational learning can affect behaviour in many ways, with both positive and negative consequences. It can teach completely new behaviours, for one. It can also increase or decrease the frequency of behaviours that have previously been learned.

Bandura emphasizes the fact that the teacher's model of social behaviour in the classroom such as calmness, friendliness, cooperativeness or aggressiveness and aloofness will act as initiator of behaviour changes in children.

The four stages of Observational Learning are:

1. Attention

We cannot learn if we are not focused on the task. If we see something as being novel or different in some way, we are likely to make it the focus of their attention. Social contexts help to reinforce these perceptions.

2. Retention

We learn by internalizing information in our memories. We recall that information later when we are required to respond to a situation that is similar the situation within which we first learned the information.

3. Production

We reproduce previously learned information (behaviour, skills, knowledge) when required. However, practice through mental and physical rehearsal often improves our responses.

4. Motivation

We need to be motivated to do anything. Often that motivation originates from our observation of someone else being rewarded or punished for something they have done or said. This usually motivates us later to do, or avoid doing, or the same thing.

Examples of Observational Learning

- An infant learns to make and understand facial expressions.
- A child learns to chew.

- After witnessing an older sibling being punished for taking a cookie without asking, the younger child does not take cookies without permission.
- A child learns to walk.
- A student learns not to cheat by watching another student be punished for cheating.

IMPORTANCE OF OBSERVATION

Observational Learning states that we learn mimetically. It is human nature to observe; we watch, listen, touch, taste and smell as part of learning. This mimetic learning theory has 4 essential factors which allow for successful Observational Learning: attention, retention, reproduction and motivation. (Laffier, 2009) The adolescent will first pay attention to the model, retain what was witnessed and then recreate the model when motivated.

The Observational Learning theory powerfully displays the importance of a strong role model who can demonstrate a preferred attitude or behaviour. From role models, adolescents are able to learn the meaning of:

- Manners
- Hard work
- Communication
- Aggression
- Production Power
- Doubt
- Motivation
- Prejudice
- Tolerance
- Confidence
- Teamwork

Educational Implications:

- Students learn a great deal simply by observing others.
- Describing the consequences of behaviour increases appropriate behaviours, decreasing inappropriate ones; this includes discussing the rewards of various behaviours.
- Modelling such as attention, retention, motor reproduction and motivation provides an alternative to teaching new behaviours.

- Students must believe that they are capable of accomplishing a task; it is important to develop a sense of self-efficacy.
- Teachers should help students set realistic expectations; ensure that expectations are realistically challenging.
- Self-regulation techniques provide an effective method for improving student behaviours.

OUT-OF-CLASSROOM LEARNING

Learning outside the classroom can be used to facilitate Education for Sustainable Development. This includes short visits into the school grounds and local community, as well as visits to farms, factories, offices, neighbourhood science centres and natural settings such as a forest, a beach or a national park.

Providing students with high quality learning activities in relevant situations beyond the walls of the classroom is vital for helping students appreciate their first hand experiences from a variety of different perspectives. An experience outside the classroom also enhances learning by providing students with opportunities to practice skills of enquiry, values analysis and clarification and problem solving in everyday situations.

However, taking students outside the classroom requires careful planning of the learning activities and attention to the health and safety risks that might be faced. This module provides guidance on these aspects of planning for learning outside the classroom.

DEFINITION

"Outdoor learning can benefit pupils of all ages and can be successful in a variety of settings... (It) enriches the curriculum and can improve educational attainment."

– Education and Skills Select Committee (2005)

Objectives:

- To develop an awareness of the positive impact that experiences outside the classroom can have on Education for Sustainable Development.

- To develop an understanding of the planning, organisation and risk management required for teaching and learning outside the classroom.
- To identify appropriate strategies for teaching and learning outside the classroom.

THE IMPORTANCE OF OUTDOOR LEARNING

In an educational context, children can be more active by being outside, they are also able to learn more freely, engage more readily and be inspired, encouraged, challenged, and therefore improve their confidence and self-esteem. These positive effects are amplified even more when it comes to an overnight camp or residential.

- Foster deeper relationships.
- Improve students' resilience, self-confidence, and well-being.
- Boost cohesion and a sense of belonging.
- Improve students' engagement with learning.
- Improve students' knowledge, skills and understanding.
- Support students' achievement.
- Smooth students' transition experiences.
- Provide opportunities for student leadership, co-design and facilitation.

THE ADVANTAGES OF TEACHING OUTSIDE

There are numerous research articles written by doctors, scientists and mental health experts explaining the benefits for children who spend more time learning outside. We have taken the points that detail the advantages of children being outside and listed them below. If you would like to read more detailed information that support these claims please follow the links at the bottom of this article.

- Children who spend more time outdoors make more friends.
- Learning outside improves attitudes to learning.
- Creates a more active imagination.

- Children who spend time outdoors are generally happier than those who stay indoors.
- Time outside increases focus on tasks.
- There are many obstacles to overcome when outdoors which boosts problem solving skills.
- Time outside improves mental wellbeing and self-esteem.
- Freedom outdoors can reduce aggression.
- It reduces obesity as children that learn to love the outdoors continue to do so in adult life.

THE DISADVANTAGES OF TEACHING OUTSIDE

There are of course disadvantages to teaching outside. These are all points that can be overcome, but they will require additional work.

- **Health & Safety regulations** - As a teacher you are responsible for the children in your class. There are certain health and safety regulation that you must follow to ensure the safety of your pupils and yourself.
- **Additional paper work** - Rise assessment plans, consent and evaluation forms will be required your school should already have school forms you can use.
- **Following curriculum requirements** - For some subjects such as maths or science it can be difficult to study outside and maintaining the curriculum requirements. It could be as simple as taking your class onto the school field.
- **Weather** - Not having the correct clothing when the weather takes a turn for the worst could prevent outdoor activities. In this case you can remind the children the day before to bring appropriate clothing for the outdoors.
- **Supervision** - The UK Department for Education state that the school is responsible for assessing and managing the risks.
- **Natural Hazards such as Bee's or uneven ground** - as long as the appropriate health and safety aspects have been adhered to you do not need to worry about these

types of accidents. It is inevitable that something will happen e.g. a child tripping over a stone. You will need to check out the area you are visiting beforehand so you will already be aware of the potential hazards.

OUT OF SCHOOL LEARNING: EXTENDING CURRICULUM LEARNING IN THE LOCAL AREA

Learning outside the classroom can be used to facilitate Education or Sustainable Development. This includes short visits into the school grounds and local community, as well as visits to farms, factories, offices, neighborhood science centers and natural settings such as a forest, beach or a national park.

Providing students with high quality learning activities in relevant situations beyond the walls of the classroom is vital for helping students appreciate their first hand experiences from a variety of different perspectives. An experience outside the classroom also enhances learning by providing students with opportunities to practice skills of enquiry, values analysis and clarification and problem solving in everyday situations.

However, taking students outside the classroom requires careful planning of the learning activities and attention to the health and safety risks that might be faced

Learning outside can be more enquiry-based and student-centered. This choice depends on the nature and objectives of the lesson. A great range of objectives can be achieved through learning outside the classroom including:

- The formation of attitudes and the development of an aesthetic awareness
- The development of understanding and knowledge
- The development of skills.

Although the teacher holds the ultimate responsibility for what happens in any lesson, the experience of learning outside the classroom can help students develop a greater sense of their own responsibilities towards each other and the tasks on which they are working.

When planning learning outside the classroom it is necessary to match the activities selected with the objectives and purposes of the field work. The selection of objectives will depend to some extent upon the timing of the fieldwork within the sequence of learning activities:

- Early in the learning sequence, learning outside the classroom may be used for basic information gathering and increasing the motivation of students.
- Towards the end of a unit of work, learning outside the classroom may be used to draw a number of themes together.
- Integrated throughout a unit of work, learning outside the classroom can develop student understanding of concepts, generalizations and principles.

CONSTRAINTS ON LEARNING OUTSIDE THE CLASSROOM

Despite the arguments in favor of learning outside the classroom, several key challenges do need to be faced:

- Organisational factors such as the difficulty of supervising a large group of students and providing them with the assistance they may need.
- The 'normal' lessons missed by teachers and students, and alterations that have to be made to the school timetable.
- Time needed to plan a worthwhile field trip.
- Cost of transport and accommodation, if required.
- Lack of detailed knowledge of the locality.
- Safety of the students.
- Lack of necessary skills in students.

Despite these challenges it should not be forgotten that often the most meaningful and lasting learning takes place when students are actively exploring the great variety of environments outside the classroom.

Learning outside the classroom also provides opportunities for teachers and students to get to know each other better through interacting outside the structures of the classroom and school grounds.

OPPORTUNITIES FOR LEARNING OUTSIDE THE CLASSROOM

Students can learn in a number of outside environments including:

- The school grounds and environs
- Urban centres
- The local community
- Rural and natural areas

There are many ways in which learning outside the classroom can be integrated into the school curriculum – not just subjects such as social studies, geography and science where fieldwork is a tradition. Languages, the arts, mathematics, business and commerce and many others also lend themselves to learning outside the classroom.

For example, in language studies, the skills of reading, writing, speaking and listening can be developed through a range of experiences outside the classroom.

1. Listening and Speaking

The School Grounds and Environs

- Listening to sounds and identifying them.
- Observing and discussing processes of decision making and conflict resolution.
- Interviewing.

The Local Community

- Visiting a police station, clinic, bank, market or park and identifying the different tones of voice that people use.
- Visiting a youth centre, and record the different types of sounds as people go about different activities.

Urban Centres

- Visiting an urban area and listening to the sounds of the city – a market, a railway station, a busy intersection, etc.
- Visiting and talking with people who live or work in the city.
- Developing a radio programme based on the sounds and voices of a town.

Rural and Natural Areas

- Listening to the sounds of a forest, the seashore or a running stream.
- Listening to the sounds on a farm. Ask the farmer to help you identify them.

2. **Reading**

The School Grounds and Environs

- Reading the notice boards in the school.

The Local Community

- Visiting the local library and using it.
- Reading material that deals with local people and places, and relating this to learners own experiences.

Urban Centres

- Reading the signs posted in town, from traffic signs to advertising.

Rural and Natural Areas

- Following written instructions for individual or group activities.
- Reading stories, poems, and non-fiction about natural history.

3. **Writing**

The School Grounds and Environs

- Compiling a school map to guide visitors.
- Writing a description of a day in the life of a typical student.

The Local Community

- Recording local data for later presentation, e.g., through role play, mime, dance, or video.
- Writing about family, community or work-related experiences.

Urban Centres

- Writing a letter to the editor of the newspaper, about a matter of current interest.

Rural and Natural Areas

- Writing a poem about your feelings while sitting in a beautiful natural area.

Approaches to learning outside the classroom:

Two common approaches are (i) Field Teaching and (ii) Field Research.

Field Teaching

- Study of topic or theme in class. Teacher talk, textbook study, note taking, slide viewing, videos, etc.
- Field observations (often teacher directed). Recording of information in the field. Some field interpretation.
- Back in the classroom – further interpretation and explanation together – writing up field report.

This is the traditional approach to teaching and learning outside the classroom. It involves taking students to a field location and delivering a mini-lecture from which students are expected to take notes. Little opportunity exists for student input and reaction. When done well, this approach can involve students in the careful observation and description of a scene or activity and in suggesting possible explanations based on previously acquired information.

This approach is useful if students are inexperienced in making their own observations or if they lack confidence in their ability to solve problems. This approach provides a structured way for them to find their own examples as an integral part of the learning experience.

Field Research

- Identification of a problem as the result of direct observations; or from class work; or from special interests of students.
- Formulation of a hypothesis as a result of reading, discussion, thinking.
- Field activities to collect data to test hypothesis.
- Data analysis – processing information.

- Hypothesis testing – accept or reject.
- Discussing and writing up of possible ways to solve the originally identified problem using information gathered in the field.

This approach represents an inductive approach to learning. It involves observation, description and explanation but with a problem solving focus. Students often use techniques similar to those used in historical enquiry, geographical research or scientific explanation. This is the inductive approach to fieldwork.

EXHIBITION

An exhibition, in the most general sense, is an organized presentation and display of a selection of items. In practice, exhibitions usually occur within museums, galleries and exhibition halls and World's fair.

The exhibition in the science fair may be classified as follows:

- Models-working and static
- Improvised apparatus
- Improved type of apparatus
- Experiments, both individual and group work
- Graphics, charts, diagrams, etc.
- Specimens, preserved or alive collection
- Demonstration – photography, silk-screen printing.

Characters

- It must safe and secure
- It must be visible
- It must catch the eye
- It must look good
- It must hold the attention
- It must be worthwhile
- It must be in good taste.

Advantages

- Raise awareness
- Meet in person
- Networking
- Launch new product
- Build your database.

Disadvantages

- Costs
- Competition
- Results aren't guaranteed
- Potential low turnouts.

MUSEUM

A museum is an institution that cares for a collection of artifacts and other objects of artistic, cultural, historical, or scientific importance. Many public museums make these items available for public viewing through exhibits that may be permanent or temporary. There are many types of museums including art museums, natural history museums, science museums, war museums and children's museums.

Uses

- Students can be motivated to collect organisms for museum
- Students spend their time usefully
- Students gain some knowledge
- Students develop the group feeling and to work co-operatively.

EXCURSION

An excursion is a trip by a group of people, usually made for leisure, education or physical purposes. It is often an adjunct to a longer journey or visit to a place, sometimes for other purposes. Short excursions for education or for observations of natural phenomena are called field trips. One-day educational field studies are often made by classes as extracurricular exercises, e.g. to visit a natural or geographical feature.

The purpose of the trip is usually observation for education, non-experimental research or to provide students with experiences outside their everyday activities, such as going camping with teachers and their classmates.

Field trips are most often done in 3 steps: preparation, activities and follow-up activity. Preparation applies to both the student and the teacher. Teachers often take the time to learn about the destination and the subject before the trip. Activities that happen on the field trips often include: lectures, tours, worksheets, videos and demonstrations. Follow-up activities are generally discussion that occurs in the classroom once the field trip is completed.

Advantages

- They provide direct source of knowledge and acquaint the student with first hand information.
- They provide an opportunity to the student for development of his aesthetic sense.
- By such excursion students become interested in the exploration of their environment.
- They help to develop in students a love for nature and to acquaint them with the real happiness in the outside world.
- It helps in development of power of observations, exploration, judgment and drawing inferences, problem solving ability of students.
- It helps in developing qualities of resourcefulness, self-confidence, initiative and leadership amongst students.
- It helps in developing cooperative attitude and various others.
- It helps in proper utilization of leisure.
- It motivates the students for self-study and self-activity.
- It helps in the development of creative faculties of the students.

Disadvantage

- Budget restraints.

- Lack of chairperson.
- Difficulty of controlling student behavior.
- Organizing an engaging lesson.
- Dealing with anxious children are potential challenges.

The Main Benefits/Advantages of Learning outside the Classroom

Learning became primarily theoretical, pictures and representations of the world instead of the world itself. But as these benefits show, it's high time more schools got back to the way we were.

- **Improved Attendance** - it has been suggested by research that Learning outside the Classroom environment improves a child's attendance, as it incentives them into more participation in the education process. By offering a method of learning that seems more engaging, then truancy levels can be cut.
- **Building For Later Life** - for older students, the chance to take part in work experience is an extremely valuable way of learning outside the classroom because it helps them to get an idea of what kind of work place environment that they would be comfortable in, and therefore can help to push them in the right direction, or prevent them from making a decision they would later regret.
- **Context** - taking students to a relevant attraction or establishment that is related to the subject that you are discussing can be a huge step towards helping them get a better grasp of the subject material. For example, somewhere like Eden Camp looks to recreate world war two, whereas a science centre contextualizes science that can't be done in a classroom.
- **Behavior** - although there's a certain risk element in taking children with behavioral problems on a school trip, research has also showed that it can have a positive effect to put them in an environment that is different and potentially far more stimulating.

- **Residential School Trips** - this type of Learning outside the Classroom is beneficial in different ways to most, as it helps to provide a lot more opportunity for combining learning about things that are on the curriculum, with broader but vitally important skills such as teamwork and communications.
- Learning outside the Classroom supports the development of healthy and active lifestyles by offering children opportunities for physical activity, freedom and movement and promoting a sense of well-being.
- Learning outside the Classroom gives children contact with the natural world and offers them experiences that are unique to outdoors, such as direct contact with the weather and the seasons.
- Playing and learning outside also help children to understand and respect nature, the environment and the interdependence of humans, animals, plants and lifecycles.
- Outdoor play also supports children's problem-solving skills and nurtures their creativity, as well as providing rich opportunities for their developing imagination, inventiveness and resourcefulness.
- Children need an outdoor environment that can provide them with space, both upwards and outwards, and places to explore, experiment, discover, be active and healthy, and to develop their physical capabilities.
- The outdoor environment offers space and therefore is particularly important to those children who learn best through active movement. Very young children learn predominantly through their sensory and physical experiences which supports brain development and the creation of neural networks.
- For many children, playing outdoors at their early years setting may be the only opportunity they have to play safely and freely while they learn to assess risk and develop the skills to manage new situations.

- Learning that flows seamlessly between indoors and outdoors makes the most efficient use of resources and builds on interests and enthusiasms.
- Anyone who takes children outside regularly sees the enjoyment and sense of wonder and excitement that is generated when children actively engage with their environment.

CONCLUSION

Learning inside the school is a concept of traditional but it adopts the natural way of learning. For the budding children inside learning helps a lot to learn abundant in naturally. Students learn new and newer things only in school setting with the help of the teachers and with models. School is where we have our first experience of formal learning, and how things go for us here can affect how we learn throughout our lives. And in order for a child to develop to their full potential, learning outside the classroom is an important way to augment the lessons taught in school. Both parents and schools can help this, and every opportunity that can be taken up, should be. Work experience is an area that should definitely be encouraged, as it allows young people to see what kind of career path they wish to take. The learning outside the classroom manifesto is a document that outlines the importance of external learning and outlines the best way to help get your students to get the best from their time with you as their teacher. So as above said both learning in and out of school must be needed for the development of student.

QUESTIONS

1. What is the purpose of learning in school?
2. Write a note on observation out of school learning.
3. Bring out the merits of learning out of school.
4. What are the approaches that enhance outside learning?
5. Explain the merits and demerits of learning in and out of school.

9

Teacher – Student Relationship

INTRODUCTION

The teacher-Student Relationship is one of the most powerful elements within the learning environment. A major factor affecting students' development, school engagement and academic motivation, teacher-student relationships form the basis of the social context in which learning takes place. Teacher-student interactions are not only influenced by a number of aspects including gender, but in turn also influence a student's academic outcomes and behaviour. Supportive and positive relationships between teachers and students ultimately promote a "sense of school belonging" and encourage students to "participate cooperatively in classroom activities".

MEANING

Teacher Student relationship is very significant in the process of teaching learning. Teachers should be imparting knowledge with concern and care to the students. Teacher's role is to guide and to reflect good character. He is like a beacon and ladder to lead the students in the right path. Student should be a receptacle to receive the knowledge given by the teacher. Students also should be submissive and obliging always to the teacher.

Teacher must take active role in the classroom activities and seek to understand and direct the students' interest in order to link with subject matter so that, learning will be a sustainable one. Teacher must also bring out the interest among children that underlie the sustainable involvement in teaching. The main task of the teachers is to search for meaningful teaching activities and to create a situation in which the child is willing to project himself into an activity so as to bring his own innate resources and innate sense of orderliness into play. The important task of the teacher is to create an environment that will support students' initiated learning.

DEFINITION

- The teacher student relationship is very important for children. ... A teacher and student who have the qualities of good communications, respect in a classroom, and show interest in teaching from the point of view of the teacher and learning from a student will establish a positive relationship in the classroom.
- Teacher-student relationships are typically defined with respect to emotional support as perceived by the student and examined with respect to their impact on student outcomes. *- Wentzel, 2009.*
- No significant learning occurs without a significant relationship. *- Dr. James Comer*
- "The strength of our student relationships makes the difference in translating our passion for teaching into their passion for learning." *- Beth Morrow*

STUDENT-TEACHER RELATIONSHIP

If a teacher has a good relationship with students, then students more readily accept the rules and procedures and the disciplinary actions that follow their violations. Without the foundation of a good relationship, students commonly resist rules and procedures along with the consequent disciplinary actions. Product also of good teacher-student relationship is responsible communication between them. The tips to maintain positive teacher-student relationship are as follows:

- Show your pleasure and enjoyment of students.
- Interact with students in a responsive and respectful manner.
- Offer students help (e.g., answering questions in timely manner, offering support that matches students' needs) in achieving academic and social objectives.
- Help students reflect on their thinking and learning skills.
- Know and demonstrate knowledge about individual students' backgrounds, interests, emotional strengths and academic levels.
- Teachers seldom show irritability or aggravation toward students.

DOS AND DON'TS

Do

- Make an effort to get to know each student in your classroom. Always call them by their names and strive to understand what they need to succeed in school.
- Make an effort to spend time individually with each student, especially those who are difficult or shy. This will help you create a more positive relationship with them.
- Be aware of the explicit and implicit messages you are giving to your students. Be careful to show your students that you want them to do well in school through both actions and words.
- Create a positive climate in your classroom by focusing not only on improving your relationships with your students, but also on enhancing the relationships among your students.

Don't

- Don't assume that being kind and respectful to students is enough to bolster their achievement. Ideal classrooms have more than a single goal: in ideal classrooms, teachers hold their students to appropriately high standards of academic performance and offer students an opportunity for an emotional connection to their teachers, their fellow students and the school.

- Don't give up too quickly on your efforts to develop positive relationships with difficult students. These students will benefit from a good teacher-student relationship as much or more than their easier-to-get-along-with peers.
- Don't assume that respectful and sensitive interactions are only important to elementary school students. Middle and high school students benefit from such relationships as well.
- Don't assume that relationships are inconsequential. Some research suggests that preschool children who have a lot of conflict with their teachers show increases in stress hormones when they interact with these teachers.

Importance of Student-Teacher relationship

- A strong student teacher relationship can make all the difference in how successful a student is.
- When the student likes and respects the teacher, he/she will be more willing to learn from them.
- When a teacher likes and respects a student, he/she is more likely to get a positive response from the student and therefore making the student more successful and the teacher getting more job satisfaction and contentment.

Need for maintaining teacher- student relationships with Students

- Enhances student achievement.
- Boosts mutual understanding.
- Breaks negative cycles.
- Promotes social-emotional learning.
- Provides an individualized intervention.
- Fosters understanding, trust and empathy.
- Benefits all members of a school community.

SUGGESTIONS FOR MAINTAINING TEACHER- STUDENT RELATIONSHIPS WITH STUDENTS

The best teachers are capable of maximizing the learning potential of every student in their class. They understand that the key to unlocking student potential is by developing positive, respectful relationships with their students beginning on the first day of the school year. Building a trusting relationship with your students can be both challenging and time-consuming. Great teachers become masters at it in time.

They will tell you that developing solid relationships with your students is paramount in fostering academic success.

It is essential that you earn your students' trust early on in the year. A trusting classroom with mutual respect is a thriving classroom complete with active, engaging learning opportunities. Some teachers are more natural at building and sustaining positive relationships with their students than others. However, most teachers can overcome a deficiency in this area by implementing a few simple strategies into their classroom on a daily basis. Here are some strategies to try:

- **Provide Structure**

Most kids respond positively to having structure in their classroom. It makes them feel safe and leads to increased learning. Teachers who lack structure not only lose valuable instructional time but often never gain the respect of their students. It is essential that teachers set the tone early by establishing clear expectations and practicing class procedures.

It is equally critical that students see that you follow through when boundaries are overstepped. Finally, a structured classroom is one with minimal downtime. Each day should be loaded with engaging learning activities with little to no downtime.

- **Teach With Enthusiasm and Passion**

Students will respond positively when a teacher is enthusiastic and passionate about the content they are teaching. Excitement is contagious! When a teacher introduces new content enthusiastically, students will buy in. They will get just as excited as the teacher, thus translating to increased learning. Exuberance will rub off on the students in your classroom when you are passionate about the content you teach.

- **Have a Positive Attitude**

Everyone has terrible days including teachers. We all go through personal trials that can be difficult to handle. It is essential that your personal issues do not interfere with your ability to teach. Teachers should approach their class each day with a positive attitude. Positivity is transcending. If the teacher is positive, the students will generally be positive. Who likes to be around someone that is always negative? Students will in time have resentment for a teacher who is always negative. However, they will run through a wall for a teacher is positive and continuously offering praise.

- **Incorporate Humour into Lessons**

Teaching and learning should not be boring. Most people love to laugh. Teachers should incorporate humour into their daily lessons. This may be sharing an appropriate joke related to the content you will be teaching that day.

It may be getting into character and donning a silly costume for a lesson. It may be laughing at yourself when you make a silly mistake. Humour comes in several forms and students will respond to it. They will enjoy coming to your class because they love to laugh and learn.

- **Make Learning Fun**

Learning should be fun and exciting. Nobody wants to spend time in a classroom where lecturing and note-taking are the norms. Students love creative, engaging lessons that grab their attention and allow them to take ownership in the learning process. Students enjoy hands-on, kinaesthetic learning activities where they can learn by doing. They are enthusiastic about technology-based lessons that are both active and visual. Students love teachers who incorporate creative, fun, engaging activities into their daily classroom.

- **Use Student Interests to your Advantage**

Every student has a passion for something. Teachers should use these interests and passions to their advantage by incorporating them into their lessons. Student surveys are a fantastic way to measure these interests. Once you know what your class is interested in, you have to find creative ways to integrate them into your lessons. Teachers who take the time to do this will see increased participation, higher involvement, and an overall increase in learning. Students will appreciate the extra effort you have made to include their interest in the learning process.

- **Incorporate Story Telling into Lessons**

Everyone loves a compelling story. Stories allow students to make real-life connections to the concepts that you are learning. Telling stories to introduce or reinforce concepts bring those concepts to life. It takes the monotony out of learning rote facts. It keeps students interested in learning. It is especially powerful when you can tell a personal story related to a concept being taught. A good story will allow students to make connections that they may not have made otherwise.

- **Show an Interest in their Lives Outside of School**

It is necessary to understand that your students have lives away from your classroom. Talk to them about their interests and extracurricular activities that they participate in. Take an interest in their interests even if you do not share the same passion. Attend a few ball games or extracurricular activities to show your support.

Encourage your students to take their passions and interests and to turn them into a career. Finally, be considerate when assigning homework. Think about the extra-curricular activities occurring on that particular day and try not to overburden your students.

- **Treat them with Respect**

Your students will never respect you if you do not respect them. You should never yell, use sarcasm, single a student out, or attempt to embarrass them. Those things will lead to a loss of respect from the entire class. Teachers should handle situations professionally. You should deal with problems individually, in a respectful, yet direct and authoritative manner. Teachers must treat each student the same. You cannot play favourites. The same set of rules must apply to all students. It is also vital that a teacher is fair and consistent when dealing with students.

- **Go the Extra Mile**

Some students need teachers who will go that extra mile to ensure that they are successful. Some teachers provide extra tutoring on their own time before and/or after school for struggling students. They put together extra work packets, communicate with parents more frequently, and take a genuine interest in the well-being of the student. Going the extra mile may mean donating clothing, shoes, food, or other household goods that a family needs to survive. It may be continuing to work with a student even after they are no longer in your classroom. It is about recognizing and assisting in meeting student needs inside and outside of the classroom.

Here are ten practical and easy ways to improve teacher-student relationships:

- Get to know the students by name as quickly as possible
- Get to know some personal things about each student
- Conduct a values analysis discussion about some current event or topic
- Provide positive comments when appropriate
- Be positive and enthusiastic when teaching
- Show students that you are not only interested in them but also that you care about them
- Avoid the use of threats and punishment
- Do not play favorites
- Create a supportive classroom environment
- Create an environment where questions and answers-even wrong answers-are encouraged and valued

AN INTERPERSONAL APPROACH TO CLASSROOM MANAGEMENT

An Interpersonal Approach to Classroom Management engages you from the start by contrasting how two teachers respond differently to common situations. The authors expertly bridge the gap between educational psychology and peer and student-teacher management from the perspectives of student engagement, classroom relationships, and teacher self regulation. Both current and prospective teachers will find helpful tools for engaging difficult students, managing challenging relationships, and handling conflict. Key topics include:

- Student behavioural, relational, and cognitive engagement in the learning process
- Classroom structures that contribute to student engagement
- The contribution of peer relationships to positive and negative behaviour management
- Strategies that help children learn to manage their own behaviour
- Connecting with students who are culturally and linguistically diverse

This practitioner-friendly guide takes you on an enlightening journey that will help you manage by design rather than by default. The results—improved relationships and enhanced learning—will not just make a difference; they will make *all* the difference.

FIVE LEVELS OF STUDENT ENGAGEMENT

It should not surprise anyone to know that one of the most consistent findings in educational research demonstrates that the more times students spend engaged during instruction, the more they learn. Some researchers even identify differing levels of engagement. Schlechty (2002) defines five levels of student engagement:

- **Authentic Engagement -** students are immersed in work that has clear meaning and immediate value to them (reading a book on a topic of personal interest)
- **Ritual Compliance** - the work has little or no immediate meaning to students, but there are extrinsic outcomes of value that keep them engaged (earning grades necessary for college acceptance)

- **Passive Compliance** - students see little or no meaning in the assigned work but expend effort merely to avoid negative consequences (not having to stay in during recess to complete work)
- **Retreatism** - students are disengaged from assigned work and make no attempt to comply, but are not disruptive to the learning of others
- **Rebellion** - students refuse to do the assigned task, act disruptive, and attempt to substitute alternative activities

MEASURING ENGAGEMENT IN THE CLASSROOM

The level of student engagement can vary from student to student, and lesson to lesson so it may be difficult to get a general feel for how engaged a class is as a whole. To that end, Schlechty (2002) also outlined three categories that can be used to measure the level of engagement for an entire classroom.

- **The Engaged Classroom**

In the engaged classroom you will observe that all students are authentically engaged at least some of the time or that most students are authentically engaged most of the time. Passive compliance and retreatism is rarely observed and rebellion is non-existent.

- **The Compliant Classroom**

The compliant classroom is the picture of traditional education. This type of classroom is orderly and most students will appear to be working so it would be easy to infer that learning is taking place. However, while there is little evidence of rebellion, retreatism is a very real danger as it is very common in the compliant classroom.

- **The Off-Task Classroom**

Retreatism and rebellion are easily observed in the off-task classroom. This type of classroom is each-student-for-them-self so you will see some degree of authentic and ritual engagement, along with passive compliance as well. Teachers in the off-task classroom spend most of their time dealing with rebelling students rather than teaching lessons that engage.

STRATEGIES FOR IMPROVING STUDENT ENGAGEMENT IN LEARNING

Why do we want learners of all ages to be engaged during instruction? Because involved students learn more efficiently and are more successful at remembering what they learned. In addition, students who are engaged in learning are more likely to become passionate about learning in general. Student engagement is one byproduct of effective instruction that has major pay offs. Now that you know how to measure your students' level of engagement, how can you increase the amount of time that students in your class are engaged in your instruction? Here are some suggestions:

1. **Use the 10:2 methods:** For every 10 minutes of instruction allow the students 2 minutes to process and respond to the instruction. This can be done in various ways by having them write what they have learned, questions they may have, or by discussing the content with a fellow student.
2. **Incorporate movement into your lessons:** Require students to respond to a question by moving to a certain spot in the room, writing on whiteboards, or standing (or sitting) when they are done thinking about the question, etc.
3. **Pick up the pace:** One misconception is that we must go slowly for students to really understand and engage in a lesson. There is a lot of evidence that shows that when teaching is at a brisk instructional pace, students have more opportunities to engage, respond, and move on to the next concept.
4. **Provide frequent and effective feedback.**
5. **Allow students 5-7 seconds of 'think time' when asking a question.** At the end of the time draw a random name to answer the question.
6. **At the end of a lesson have students use the 3-2-1 method of summarizing** by having students record three things they learned, two interesting things, and one question they have about what was taught. Allow time to share their findings with a peer.

7. **Periodically pause mid-sentence** when teaching requiring students to fill in the blanks.

CLASSROOM MANAGEMENT

Classroom management has been defined broadly as any action a teacher takes to create an environment that supports and facilitates both academic and social-emotional learning facilitates both academic and social-emotional learning. Instructional procedures could also be considered classroom management by this definition; however, effective instruction alone is insufficient for establishing universal classroom management. Procedures that structure the classroom environment, encourage appropriate behaviour, and reduce the occurrence of inappropriate behaviour are necessary for strong classroom management.

Effective classroom management focuses on preventive rather than reactive procedures and establishes a positive classroom environment in which the teacher focuses on students who behave appropriately. Rules and routines are powerful preventative components to classroom organization and management plans because they establish the behavioural context of the classroom by specifying what is expected, what will be reinforced, and what will be retaught if inappropriate behaviour occurs. This prevents problem behaviour by giving students specific, appropriate behaviours to engage in. Monitoring student behaviour allows the teacher to acknowledge students who are engaging in appropriate behaviour and prevent misbehaviour from escalating.

The components of effective classroom management are important in several ways. The main components are:

1. Organizing the classroom;
2. Planning and teaching rules and procedures;
3. Managing student work and improving student accountability;
4. Maintaining good student behaviour;
5. Planning and organizing;

6. Conducting instruction and maintaining momentum; and
7. Getting the year off to a good start.

HEALTHY CLASSROOM MANAGEMENT

Classroom Management refers to the wide variety of skills and techniques and that teachers use to keep students organized, orderly, focused, attentive, on task and academically productive during a class. When Classroom Management strategies are excited effectively, teachers minimize the behaviours that impede learning for both individual students and group of students while minimizing the behaviours that facilitate or enhance learning. Generally speaking, effective teachers tend to display strong classroom-management skills. The interest and the attention of the learners to make them actively participate in all the activities related to classroom activities could be gained only by healthy classroom management. It extends to everything that learners may do to facilitate or improve student learning, which would include factors such as:

- **Behaviour** - A positive attitude, happy facial expressions, encouraging statements the respectful and fair treatment of students, etc.
- **Environment** - A welcoming ventilated well-lit classroom filled with intellectually stimulating learning materials that's organized to support specific learning activities.
- **Expectations** - the quality of work that teacher expect students to produce, the ways that teacher expect student to behave to word other students, the agreements that teachers make its students.
- **Materials** - the type of texts, equipments, etc.
- **Learning resources or activities** - the kinds of learning experiences that teacher design to engage student interest, passions and intellectual curiosity.

We should note that poorly designed lessons, uninteresting learning materials or unclear expectations could contribute to greater student disinterest, increased behavioural problems, or unruly and disorganised classes.

Healthy classroom cannot be easily separated from all the other decisions that teachers make. Some of the technique could be adopted by the teachers for maintaining healthy classroom management are as follows,

- **Entry Routine:** It is a technique in which the teacher establish a consistent, daily routine that begins as soon as entre the classroom like preparing learning materials, making seating arrangements, passing in homework or doing a brief physical warm up activity. This activity can avoid the disorder and squandered time that can characterize the beginning of a class period.
- **Do now written activity:** It is a written activity that students are given as soon as they arrive in the classroom. This technique is intended to get students settled, focused, productive, and prepared for instruction as quick as possible.
- **Tight transitions:** It is a technique in which teachers establish transitions routines that students learn and can execute quickly and repeatedly without much direction from a teacher. This technique helps to maximise instructional time by reducing the delay that might accompany transitions between activities.
- **Seat signals:** It is a technique in which students use nonverbal signals while seated to indicate that they need something such as help with a problem or a restroom break, etc.
- **Applaud up:** It is an act of publicity recognizing and praising students who have done something good such as answering a difficult question or helping a peer, etc.
- **Non-verbal Interventions:** Is when teachers establish eye contact or make gestures that let students know that they are not paying attention or misbehaving.
- **Positive group correction:** It is a quick, affirming verbal reminder that lets a group of students knows what they should be doing.

- **Public Correction:** It is a quick, positive reminder that tells on individual student what do to instead of what not do to. This is intended to establish a group culture in which learning accomplishments and positive actions are socially valued and rewarded. Healthy classroom management has received an increasing amount of attention from education leaders, reformers and researchers, who have begun to investigate, analyse and document the effective strategies used by successful teachers. The growing emphasis on classroom management and that strong management skill are foundations of strong teaching.

ACADEMIC ACHIEVEMENT

Academic achievement or (academic) performance is the extent to which a student, teacher or institution has achieved their short or long-term educational goals. Cumulative GPA and completion of educational degrees such as High School and bachelor's degrees represent academic achievement. When students feel safe, engaged, and respected, they can focus on their academic goals. Effective character educators ensure that these needs are met. Character education is the foundation upon which students can reach academic achievement. It's not just about teaching kids to be good. It's teaching them to be their best.

Academic achievement is commonly measured through examinations or continuous assessments but there is no general agreement on how it is best evaluated or which aspects are most important — procedural knowledge such as skills or declarative knowledge such as facts. Furthermore, there are inconclusive results over which individual factors successfully predict academic performance, elements such as test anxiety, environment, motivation, and emotions require consideration when developing models of school achievement.

In California, the achievement of schools is measured by the Academic Performance Index.

FACTORS INFLUENCING ACADEMIC ACHIEVEMENT

- **Individual differences influencing academic performance:**

Individual differences in academic performance have been linked to differences in intelligence and personality. Students with higher mental ability as demonstrated by IQ tests and those who are higher in conscientiousness (linked to effort and achievement motivation) tend to achieve highly in academic settings. A recent meta-analysis suggested that mental curiosity (as measured by typical intellectual engagement) has an important influence on academic achievement in addition to intelligence and conscientiousness.

Children's semi-structured home learning environment transitions into a more structured learning environment when children start first grade. Early academic achievement enhances later academic achievement.

Parent's academic socialization is a term describing the way parents influence students' academic achievement by shaping students' skills, behaviours and attitudes towards school. Parents influence students through the environment and discourse parents have with their children. Academic socialization can be influenced by parents' socio-economic status. Highly educated parents tend to have more stimulating learning environments. Further, recent research indicates that the relationship quality with parents will influence the development of academic self-efficacy among adolescent-aged children, which will in turn affect their academic performance.

Children's first few years of life are crucial to the development of language and social skills. School preparedness in these areas help students adjust to academic expectancies.

Indirect evidence suggests that physical activity could have an impact on academic achievement. Studies have shown that physical activity can increase neural activity in the brain. Exercise specifically increases executive brain functions such as attention span and working memory.

- **Cognitive Factors**

Cognitive factors or learning factors are the extent to which a person's individual capabilities can influence their academic or learning performance. These factors include cognitive functions like attention, memory, and reasoning. Cognitive factors are often measured through examinations; college admission boards use standardized tests such as the SAT and ACT when evaluating prospective candidates. Undergraduate students with high academic performance present mature learning beliefs, and a strong knowledge integration.

- **Non-Cognitive**

Non-cognitive factors or skills are a set of "attitudes, behaviours, and strategies" that promotes academic and professional success, such as academic self-efficacy, self-control, motivation, expectancy and goal setting theories, emotional intelligence, and determination. To create attention on factors other than those measured by cognitive test scores sociologists Bowles and Gintis coined the term in the 1970s. The term serves as a distinction of cognitive factors, which are measured by teachers through tests and quizzes. Non-cognitive skills are increasingly gaining popularity because they provide a better explanation for academic and professional outcomes.

- **Motivation**

Motivation is the reasoning behind an individual's actions. Research has found that students with higher academic performance, motivation and persistence use intrinsic goals rather than extrinsic ones. Furthermore, students who are motivated to improve upon their previous or upcoming performance tend to perform better academically than peers with lower motivation. In other words, students with higher need for achievement have greater academic performance.

- **Self-Control**

Self-Control, in the academic setting, is related self-discipline, self-regulation, delay of gratification and impulse control. Baumeister, Vohs, and Tice defined self-control as "the capacity for altering one's own responses, especially to bring them into line with standards such as ideals, values, morals, and social expectations, and to support the attainment of long-term goals." In other words, self-control is the ability to prioritize long-term goals over the temptation of short-term impulses. Self-control is usually measured through self completed questionnaires.

- **Extracurricular Activities**

Organized extracurricular activities have yielded a positive relationship with high academic performance including increasing attendance rates, school engagement, GPA, post secondary education, as well as a decrease in dropout rates and depression. Additionally, positive developmental outcomes have been found in youth that engage in organized extracurricular activities. High school athletics have been linked with strong academic performance, particularly among urban youth.

- **Successful Educational Actions**

There are experiences analysed by research projects that show how the incorporation of Successful Educational Actions (SEAs) in schools with high absenteeism are contributing to the improvement of academic achievement.

- **Socio-Economic Status (SES)**

Socio-economic status can be defined as 'a person's overall social position... to which attainments in both the social and economic domain contributes'. When used in studies of children's school achievement, it refers to the SES of the parents or family. Socio-economic status is determined by an individual's achievements in: education; employment and occupational status; and income and wealth. Several comprehensive reviews of the relationship between SES and educational outcomes exist. These studies and reviews make it clear those children from low SES families are more likely to exhibit the following patterns in terms of educational outcomes compared to children from high SES families:

- have lower levels of literacy, numeracy and comprehension;
- have lower retention rates;
- have lower higher education participation rates;
- exhibit higher levels of problematic school behaviour (for instance truancy);
- are less likely to study specialised maths and science subjects;
- are more likely to have difficulties with their studies and display negative attitudes to school; and
- have less successful school-to-labour market transitions.

- **Family Structure**

Socio-economic status may therefore also be linked to family structure. As sole parent families on average have lower levels of income, are headed by parents with lower educational attainment and are less likely to be in the labour force, children from these families are likely to have lower educational performance. Other factors in sole parent families that are likely to adversely affect educational outcomes of children compared to those from two-parent families are said to include:

- reduced contact between the child and non-custodial parent;
- the custodial parent having less time to spend with children in terms of supervision of school-work and maintaining appropriate levels of discipline;
- the lack of an appropriate role model, especially for males;
- increased responsibilities on children such as childcare roles, domestic duties which impede the time available for school work; and
- the nature of parent-child relationships in sole parent families may cause emotional and behavioural problems for the child.

- **Type of School**

As well as Socio-economic Status (SES), research has shown the importance of the type of school a child attends in influencing educational outcomes. SES variables continue to influence educational attainment even after controlling for different school types; the school context tends to affect the strength of the relationship between SES and educational outcomes. Students from independent private schools are also more likely to achieve higher end of school scores. While school-related factors are important, there is again an indirect link to SES, as private schools are more likely to have a greater number of students from high SES families, select students with stronger academic abilities and have greater financial resources. The school effect is also likely to operate through variation in the quality and attitudes of teachers. Teachers at disadvantaged schools, for instance, often hold low expectations of their students, which compound the low expectations students and their parents may also hold.

- **Absences**

Also related to poor educational performance is the level of truancy or unexplained absence among students. Truancy can be modelled both as an educational outcome and as a causal factor in explaining educational performance.

- **Gender**

Educational performance at school has also been found to vary according to the student's sex. In particular, reviews of the evidence suggest that boys suffer an educational disadvantage relative to girls, especially in terms of performance in literacy. There are several explanations for this increasing gender gap which include: biological differences; gender biases (such as reading being seen as 'not masculine'); teaching, curricula and assessment (for instance less structured approaches to teaching grammar may have weakened boys' literacy performance); and socioeconomic factors.

- **Geographical Location**

Students from non-metropolitan areas are more likely to have lowered educational outcomes in terms of academic performance and retention rates than students from metropolitan areas. Despite an adequate number of educational facilities in rural and remote area, school children from these areas remain disadvantaged by other factors. Issues affecting access to education in regional areas include costs, the availability of transport and levels of family income support.

- **Housing Type**

Lower educational attainment has also been found to be associated with children living in public housing compared to those in private housing. This may be due to the effects of overcrowding, poor access to resources and a lack of social networks, and in this sense, housing type may also be a measure of neighbourhood influence.

CONCLUSION

Through positive relationships, students not only learn that particular beliefs are useful for functioning in school and the classroom, they also internalize beliefs valued by significant others such as teachers and parents. Positive relationships have an energizing function on the self, working to activate positive mood and affect. Teacher-student relationships require much attention from teachers in the classroom, and are an important source of their concerns and happiness. This energy gained from positive interpersonal relationships provides an important pathway to motivation and engagement.

QUESTIONS

1. Discuss the need for maintaining teacher –student relationship.
2. Write an essay on interpersonal approach in class room management.
3. Discuss in detail the strategies for improving student engagement in learning.

4. Explain the necessity for teachers' involvement and interaction.
5. Analyze the role of Healthy classroom management and academic achievement.

10

Teaching as a Profession

INTRODUCTION

Teaching is a process that facilitates learning. Teaching is the specialized application of knowledge, skills and attributes designed to provide unique service to meet the educational needs of the individual and of the society. The choice of teaching activities varies depends upon the goals of education and the responsibility of the teachers in the teaching profession.

Teaching is a comprehensive process which involves systematic approach to accomplish the goals and aims of education. It is a goal driven process where the teacher plays an eminent role in the process. It is more than telling, but achieving behavioural changes. Teachers should be effective in their profession.

CONCEPT OF TEACHING

Teaching is a complex, goal oriented, multifaceted activity. Teaching and learning are the set of events that are designed to bring about behavioural changes in instruction. It is an event that happens outside the learners supports the internal process which modifies the behaviour of an individual through learning. Hence, teaching is an internal process of learning.

Teaching is a process which usually takes place in the classroom situations. It is a formal process through which the teacher interacts with the students to give what he/she wants the learners to learn according to their learning needs. It is a systematic way to attain some pre-determined goal. Teaching is to cause motivation to learn and to fill the minds of the learners by information knowledge of facts. It imparts understanding of concepts and basic life skills.

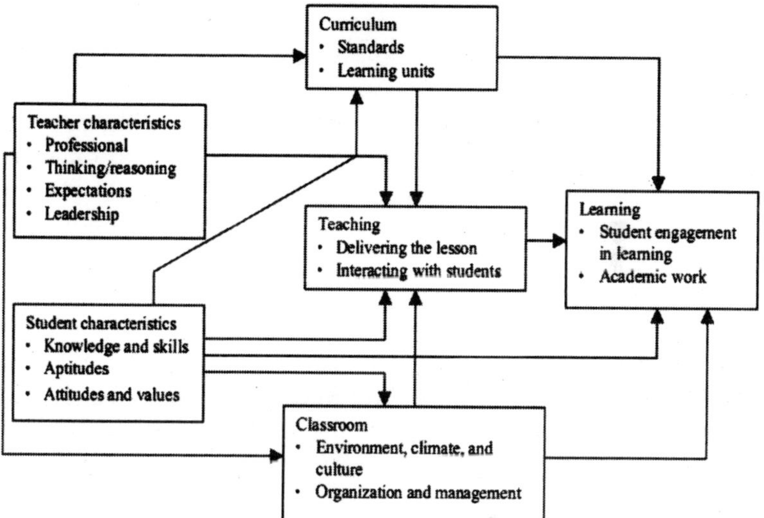

OBJECTIVES OF TEACHING

The most remarkable objectives of teaching are:

1. **All Round Development of a Learner** - The prime objective of teaching is the all round development of the learner that includes his physical, mental and spiritual or moral development. This objective is the basis of Gandhi's idea of basic education.
2. **Behaviour change** - The education should be imparted to a learner in such a way that it reflects the attitude, behaviour and personality of the learner.
3. **Development of Adjustment** - The manner of teaching should be such that it makes the pupils feel at home in his class room. The teacher has to ensure that the learner is well adjusted to the environment which includes his classmates, school mates and other members of his society at large.

4. **Learner's Mental Ability -** The teacher should take into account the mental ability of the pupils while teaching. This will enable the teacher to make him-self more communicative with his students and in turn the students will have a better understanding of what is being taught to them.
5. **Transmission of Knowledge -** The process of teaching should ensure that the knowledge is transmitted from the teacher to the pupil. For achieving this objective, the teaching need to be very communicative and the process of teaching should ensure the pupil participation in it. The more the pupils are encouraged to interact with the teacher, the more the chances of transmission of knowledge.
6. **Assimilation of Lessons** - Teaching does not stop at delivering lectures and giving home tasks to the students. It has to be responsible for the assimilation of what is taught to the students. The manner of teaching should be pleasant enough to make the students grasp whatever they are taught.
7. **Friendly Environment -** One of the primary objectives of teaching is to make the environment of the place of teaching more friendly and conducive to learning. His all attention should remain focused to the teaching and he, should not get irritated with the non-conducive atmosphere of the class room.

Principles of Teaching:

- Principle of using previous knowledge.
- Principle of providing for individual difference.
- Principle of readiness.
- Principle of meaningfulness.
- Principle defining specific objectives of the lesson.
- Principle of proceeding from simple to complex.
- Principle of proceeding from concrete to abstract.
- Principle of proceeding from general to specific.
- Principle of proceeding from known to unknown.

Functions of Teaching:

- Creating learning situations.
- Motivating the child to learn.
- Arranging for conditions which assist in the growth of the child's mind and body.
- Utilize the initiative and play urges of the children to facilitate learning.
- Turning the children with the nobility of thoughts, feelings and actions.
- Giving information and explaining it.
- Diagnosing learning problems.
- Making curricular material.
- Evaluating recording and reporting.

STEPS OF TEACHING

In order to make teaching an effective process one needs to follow certain steps. These steps are so important that these cannot be removed from the process of teaching. If a teacher deviates from these steps, the outcome of the teaching may be biased.

1. Planning

Without a plan, one cannot proceed in a resolution. In the teaching-learning process also a teacher has to make a plan according to the strength of the students, the locality of the school the environmental conditions of the school and the contents and the subjects he is going to teach. He has to take into consideration the language that he finds suitable for teaching. The planning includes the gradation of students, as to how many are present in the class, how many are absent, how many are high achieving and how many mediocre. The teacher has to plan for the arrangement of teaching aids like maps, charts, models, overhead projector etc.

2. Preparation

During the preparation stage, the teacher has to follow the subject or topic systematically. As the present times are times of science and technology, the presentation must also be scientific in nature for which the teacher may need overhead projectors, slides TV and video tapes etc. for making his presentation more effective and understandable.

3. Presentation

After preparation, the teacher is prepared to present the topic in the class to the full satisfaction of students and the observer who is there to watch his presentation.

4. Comparison

Comparison is an important characteristic of teaching. It allows a second chance, to all the three participants, the teacher, the learner and the observer to arrange one more program of teaching-learning in order to remove, any shortcomings found in the first attempt.

NATURE OF TEACHING

In its broadest sense, teaching is a process that facilitates learning. Teaching is the specialized application of knowledge, skills and attributes designed to provide unique service to meet the educational needs of the individual and of society. The choice of learning activities whereby the goals of education are realized in the school is the responsibility of the teaching profession.

In addition to providing students with learning opportunities to meet curriculum outcomes, teaching emphasizes the development of values and guides students in their social relationships. Teachers employ practices that develop positive self-concept in students. As teaching takes place in a classroom setting, the direct interaction between teacher and student is the most important element in teaching.

1. **Dynamic, Social & Humane:** Influenced by human & social factors.

To know factor affecting teaching is so important because after analysis all factors which affecting teaching, teacher can improve himself and can become good teacher and create better citizen for country. If study teaching subjects, we find many factors which affecting teaching which can write in list of these factors.

- Teacher knowledge, enthusiasm and responsibility for learning.
- Classroom activities that encourage learning.
- Assessment activities that encourage learning through experience.
- Effective feedback that establishes the learning processes in the classroom.
- Effective interaction between the teacher and the students, creating an environment that respects, encourages and stimulates learning through experience.

Human and Social factors affect the teaching are as follows:

EDUCATIONAL QUALIFICATION OF TEACHER

Higher qualified teacher can provide high scholarly instructions which can effect than general graduate teacher. Many teachers hold different degrees which is the sign of their higher education qualification. A teacher is just B.A. and other teacher is M.A., M.Ed., PhD, if we compare both, then is sure that higher qualified teacher can cede good teaching result.

SKILLS

Skill is an ability to do any work with better way. If a teacher has teaching skill then he can provide effective teaching. Often says that teaching is God gifted but getting good education training and Psychologize best educational books, we can get this skill and create better result. In teaching talent we can include following skills.

- Communication skill of teacher
- Method of teaching
- Taking teaching aids
- Human relation skill
- Technique of teaching

EXPERIENCE OF TEACHER

Experience of teacher affects also the teaching. After increasing teaching experience, a teacher learns many new things in teaching experience which he can employ in next time teaching. First day teacher may not effect on students but after 5 years teaching, a teacher can more effect on students.

CLASSROOM ENVIRONMENT

Classroom environment effects also on teaching. This environment is made both by teacher and students. Without both active participation in education, teaching never effects. If the concentration lives in class room and students listen teacher's voice and teacher also cares the activity of teacher doing interacting with students.

ECONOMIC FACTOR

Economic background of teacher and student is also affected teaching. Even salary of teacher effects on his thinking level. Poor and rich students can also classify economically and sometime these factors can effect on effective teaching.

ADMINISTRATIVE POLICIES OF SCHOOL OR COLLEGE OR UNIVERSITY

Administrative policies also effect teaching. Teacher wants to instruct with his way but administrative policies is not allowed, so the voice of teach can stop and effect of teaching may slow in class room.

SUBJECT MATTER

Sometime when a teacher teaches that subject in which he is not specialize, he cannot create any effect through his teaching but same teacher can teaches his specialize subject with better way.

PARENTAL EXPECTATIONS

What are the expectations of parent on students? This factor can be defined psychologically. If parent wants to frame up his children doctor or engineer and continually stress on student, sometime student may not at that rank, so mentally he can create depression and which can stop effective teaching of teacher.

2. **An Art & Science:** Exercise of being systematic & including talent & creativity.

Teaching as an art: The teaching is considered to an art because it involves skill to dissimilate language, to maintain the interest and attain of the learner and the decide handling of the problems of the learners to modify his behaviour. The concept of teaching as an art is the view capabilities and skills which excellent teaching demands are far loser to those required of artists. The four reasons which define teaching as an art are follows:

- It is an art in the sense that teaching can be performed with such skill and grace that, for the students as for the teacher, the experience can be justifiably characterized as aesthetic.
- Teaching is an art in the sense that teacher's, like painters, composers, actress and dancers, make judgement based on qualities that unfold during the course of action.
- Teaching is an art in the sense that the teacher's activity is not dominated by prescriptions or routines but is influenced by qualities and contingencies that are unpredicted.
- Teaching is an art in the sense that the ends it achieves are often related in process.

Teaching as a science: The teaching is an applied science because it incorporates systematic and methodological approach. The system and method, the experimentation and trial, the probing and ensuing are the basis of teaching learning process hence we can say that teaching is definitely a science. From this point on, the practices of teaching and teacher education came to seen as legitimate fields of scientific inquiry and knowledge, offering the underlying basis for ensuing educational theory and practice. The scientific perspective in the training of teachers, shape the entire approach to pre-service and in-service training. From a perspective based on attaining the best possible result in the most efficient manner, schools have increasingly been viewed as a form of service institution in which teachers are to be held accountable for productivity, often measured on the basis of their pupils standardized test scores.

3. **Diverse in Application:** There are various forms of teaching.

VARIOUS METHODS IN TEACHING

The term teaching method refers to the general principle. Pedagogy and management are the strategies used for classroom instructions. The teacher's choice of teaching method depends on what fits the learner to educational philosophy, classroom demographic, subject areas and educational goals. Teaching theories – primarily fall into two categories or 'approaches' are as follows:

(a) Teacher – centred approach

Teachers are the main authority figure in this model; students are viewed as 'empty vessels' whose primary role is to passively receive information (via lectures and direct information) with an end goal of testing and assessment. It is the primary role of teachers to pass knowledge and information on to their students. In this model teaching and assessment are viewed as two separate entitles. Student learning is measured through scored test assessment. The following are the various methods of teacher-centred methods:

- Lecture Method
- Demonstration Method
- Team Teaching Method

(b) Student – centred approach

While teachers are an authority figure in this model, teachers and students play an equally active role in the learning process. The teachers primary role is to coach facilitate learning and overall comprehension of material. Student learning is measured through both formal and informal of assessment are connected; student learning is continuously measured during teacher instruction. The following are the various methods of student-centred methods.

- Laboratory Method
- Project Method
- Assignment Method
- Heuristic Method
- Symposium Method
- Seminar Method
- Workshop Method

TEACHING AS A PROFESSION

"Teaching is a noble profession"

The word "profession" is synonymous to: Occupation, job, career, work, and line of work. The word "Professional" means long & arduous years of preparation, a striving for excellence, a dedication to public interest and commitment to moral and ethical values.

Teacher's involvement of intellectual competence, the ability to perform all their skilled service upon which continued functioning of modern society depends therefore we can say the meaning thereby that teaching is a profession. Effective teacher provide the students opportunities for learning. Teacher facilitates the instruction among the students. Teacher organizes to construct the knowledge. In short, teaching is effective to the extent that the teachers' art in ways that are favourable to the development o f basic skill, understanding work habits, desirable attitudes, and value judgements of students. Teaching profession is related to teaching job. The profession can be started at job-role of teaching. Teaching profession requires education and training and attitudes towards his students. Teaching is considered as a noble profession. There are several professions which have different job roles.

Characteristics of a profession:

- It has long term education and training for a job-role
- It should cater the needs of the society and the nation
- There should be social accountability
- There should be some ethical norms or considerations
- There should be a professional association
- There should be autonomy and self regulations
- There should be freedom to charge reasonable fee for the service.

What is teaching profession?

Teachers are the shadows of parents showing love and seldom admonishing, reaching out to be creators narrating noble deeds, like a goldsmith hammering to enrich skills and moulding tiny tots to perfection. Teaching profession is a noble one every teacher must play an important role in making a child to realize their dreams.

The Four beliefs of an Effective Teacher:

- It is the teacher who makes the difference in the classroom.
- By far the most important factor in school learning is the ability of the teacher.
- There is an extensive body of knowledge about teaching that must be known by the teacher.
- The teacher must be a decision maker able to translate the body of knowledge about teaching into increased student learning.

Professional Standards in Teaching Profession:

The teaching profession demands:

- Good communication with professional experts, colleagues and students
- Sound knowledge in the subject and related duties that is to be performed
- Technical skill of teaching explicitly and focused content orientation
- System evaluation and opening a new spectrum of information
- Firm determination & commitment with the profession of teaching
- Refined values and behavior.

SOCIAL STANDARDS IN TEACHING PROFESSION

It is a teacher who prepares students to behave appropriately within campus and in the society. Social norms and cultural values are considered part of professional and social life transferred from a teacher to student. This necessitates academia to become a role model leaving a positive impact on students in and out of the classroom. Teachers are expected to meet the following social standard code of ethics:

- Social interaction
- Good human being
- Good relations with colleagues
- Good relations with students
- Positive attitude
- Passion for public service
- Fairness in dealings
- Loyalty to country and nation.

The teaching profession fulfills those criteria in the following ways:

- Teachers have an organized body of knowledge that separates the group from all others.
- It serves a great social purpose.
- There is cooperation achieved through a professional organization.
- There is a formal period of preparation and a requirement for continuous growth and development.
- There is a degree of autonomy accorded the professional.
- The profession has control or influence over education standards, admissions, licensing, professional development, ethical and performance standards, and professional discipline.

EFFECTIVE TEACHING

It is difficult to define "effective teaching"— people with completely different styles are equally effective. The one thing that we have learned in research in higher education is that there is no one best way of teaching.

Vogt (1984) related effective teaching to the ability to provide instruction to different students of different abilities while incorporating instructional objectives and assessing the effective learning mode of the students.

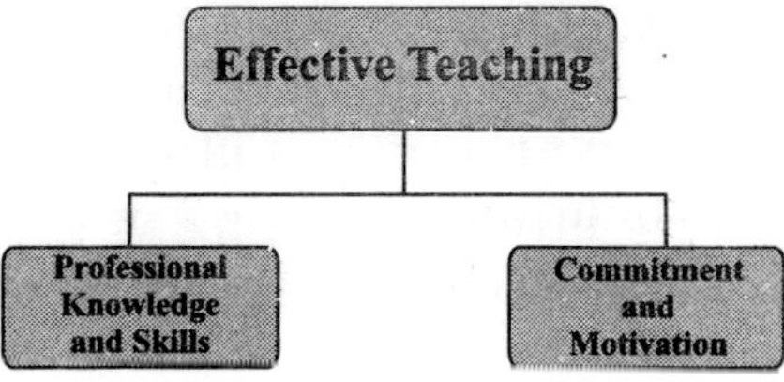

PROFESSIONAL KNOWLEDGE AND SKILLS

Effective Teachers:

- Use effective strategies to promote students' motivation to learn
- Communicate well with students and parents
- Work effectively with students from culturally diverse backgrounds
- Have good assessment skills
- Integrate technology into the curriculum
- Exhibit subject matter competence
- Implement appropriate instructional strategies
- Set high goals for themselves and students and plan for instruction
- Create developmentally appropriate instructional materials and activities
- Manage classrooms for optimal learning

COMMITMENT AND MOTIVATION

Effective Teachers

- Have a good attitude
- Care about students
- Invest time and effort
- Bring a positive attitude and enthusiasm to the classroom

Seven Principles of Effective Teaching:

1. Effective teaching involves acquiring relevant knowledge about students and using that knowledge to inform our course design and classroom teaching.
2. Effective teaching involves aligning the three major components of instruction: learning objectives, assessments, and instructional activities.
3. Effective teaching involves articulating explicit expectations regarding learning outcomes and policies.
4. Effective teaching involves prioritizing the knowledge and skills we choose to focus on.

5. Effective teaching involves recognizing and overcoming our expert blind spots.
6. Effective teaching involves adopting appropriate teaching roles to support our learning goals.
7. Effective teaching involves progressively refining our courses based on reflection and feedback.

Characteristics of Effective teaching:

1. Begins class promptly and in a well-organized way.
2. Treats students with respect and caring.
3. Provides the significance/importance of information to be learned.
4. Provides clear explanations. Holds attention and respect of students....practices effective classroom management.
5. Uses active, hands-on student learning.
6. Varies his/her instructional techniques.
7. Provides clear, specific expectations for assignments.
8. Provides frequent and immediate feedback to students on their performance.
9. Praises student answers and uses probing questions to clarify/elaborate answers.
10. Provides many concrete, real-life, practical examples.
11. Draws inferences from examples/models....and uses analogies.
12. Creates a class environment which is comfortable for students....allows students to speak freely.
13. Teaches at an appropriately fast pace, stopping to check student understanding and engagement.
14. Communicates at the level of all students in class.
15. Has a sense of humour!
16. Uses nonverbal behaviour, such as gestures, walking around, and eye contact to reinforce his/her comments.
17. Presents him/herself in class as "real people."
18. Focuses on the class objective and does not let class get sidetracked.

19. Uses feedback from students (and others) to assess and improve teaching.
20. Reflects on own teaching to improve it.

Characteristics of Ineffective teaching:

1. **Disrespect students.** If you give students a sense that you don't respect them, the class will probably be a bad experience for everyone no matter what else you do, while if you clearly convey respect and caring, it will cover a multitude of pedagogical sins you might commit.
2. **Teach without clear learning objectives.** A key to making courses coherent and tests fair is to write learning objectives-explicit statements of what students should be able to do if they have learned what the instructor wants them to learn-and to use the objectives as the basis for designing lessons, assignments, and exams.
3. **Get stuck in a rut.** Things are always happening that provide incentives and opportunities for improving courses. This is not to say that you have to make major revisions in your course every time you give it-you probably don't have time to do that, and there's no reason to. Rather, just keep your eyes open for possible improvements you might make in the time available to you.
4. **Give tests that are too long.** If you want to evaluate your students' potential to be successful professionals, test their mastery of the knowledge and skills you are teaching, not their problem-solving speed.
5. **Fail to establish relevance.** To provide better motivation, begin the course by describing how the content relates to important technological and social problems and to whatever you know of the students' experience, interests, and career goals, and do the same thing when you introduce each new topic.
6. **Have students work in groups with no individual accountability.** The way to make group work is cooperative learning, an exhaustively researched

instructional method that effectively promotes development of both cognitive and interpersonal skills

7. **Fail to provide variety in instruction.** Effective instruction mixes things up: board-work, multimedia, storytelling, discussion, activities, individual assignments, and group work. The more variety you build in, the more effective the class is likely to be.
8. **Turn classes into PowerPoint shows.** Droning through lecture notes put into PowerPoint slides is generally a waste of time for everyone.
9. **Call on student's cold.** If you frequently call on students without giving them time to think ("cold-calling"), the ones who are intimidated by it won't be following your lecture as much as praying that you don't land on them. Even worse, as soon as you call on someone, the others breathe a sigh of relief and stop thinking.
10. **When you ask a question in class, immediately call for volunteers.** When you do this most students will avoid eye contact, and either you get a response from one of the two or three who always volunteer or you answer your own question.
11. **Never Using Visuals.** Less-effective teachers only lecture and never use visuals to accompany their lessons. Most students prefer to learn through a hands-on approach, or need to be visually stimulated to help them make a connection to what they are learning. Lecturing and text-driven teaching usually doesn't serve students well. Visuals give students a chance to physically see what you are talking about.
12. **Asking for Volunteers before they ask a Question.** Most students do not respond well (expect may be your select few) when a teacher asks for volunteers to answer a question. Do not say, "I need a volunteer to answer this question: Who was the 10th President of the United States?" If you do this, you will only get the same few people who always raise their hands, as well as a

classroom full of students who are avoiding eye contact with you because they do not want to answer your question.

13. **Making Students Always Take Notes.** Taking notes is a great hands-on way to keep students involved in what you are teaching them, while you are teaching. But if note taking becomes the only way that you teach, and students are always just copying what you have written on the board, they will become extremely bored and unengaged. Try giving students an outline of the notes that you want them to take so they are actively involved. They can fill in the blanks as you speak and get a chance to participate while you are teaching.
14. **Failing to Mix it up.** Less-effective teachers are monotonous in their teaching, and always teach the same boring lessons in the same boring way, year after year. These teachers never mix it up and try new things. Variety is the spice of life, which means that an effective teacher knows that the more variety you have in your activities, the more likely your students will be engaged.
15. **Never Using Cooperative Learning.** Cooperative learning is the "Super Bowl" of group work. It gives each group member individual accountability in order for their group to succeed in their task. While many teachers love to put students into groups because they think it's a great way for them to learn, ineffective teachers fail to realize that each student needs to be accountable for themselves as well as their group work, and that is just what cooperative learning does.
16. **Giving too Many Tests, or Too Long Tests.** Assessing students' work is an important part of learning, but your goal is to test their knowledge and skills, not speed or how many tests they can master. A 10-question test can be just as effective in determining the mastery of their skills as a 50-question test. Keep tests short and conduct them about once a week.

17. **Being Disrespectful to Students.** Just as you want to be treated with respect, so do your students. Far too often, teachers take their role as an authority figure too far, and forget to treat their students with respect because they think they are older and wiser. While this may hold true, it is still important to treat others as you want to be treated if you want your students to enjoy your class.
18. **Failing to Connect Content to the Real World.** Student motivation begins with student interest and connecting what you are teaching with the real world. Ineffective teachers fail to establish relevance that relates to what students know and see every day. Successful teachers know that they need to find out students' interests and goals, and take that and connect it to what they are teaching and make it relevant to their lives.

TEACHING – THE MOST IMPORTANT PROFESSION:

"It appears, therefore, that of all secular professions, teaching is the most profoundly important..." "Of all these professions teaching is the worse paid."

- Teachers have the capacity to shape the minds and futures of many - and they do so at all kinds of critical life stages.
- Kindergarten teachers introduce young minds to the wonder of learning - and to the basic tools of learning that students will use their entire lives.
- Middle School teachers have the challenge of instilling a passion for academics in large groups of teens whose minds are so deeply focused on developmental issues and their social worlds.
- High school teachers are charged with teaching detailed intellectual content to large groups of "near adults" - whose worlds are often tumultuous on the inside and on the outside.
- College professors are charged with inspiring young adults - teaching them the nuts-and-bolts of highly technical content areas while showing them how limitless their life possibilities are.

- And in combination, across an individual's lifespan, it is an army of teachers who have ultimately shaped how that individual understands the world and his or her place in it.

Reasons Why Teaching is the best Profession:

1. The potential to transform lives.
2. It gives you the chance to be continuously creative.
3. It offers you a chance to continuously get better.
4. It is grounding, humbling profession.
5. There is always satisfaction somewhere.
6. It's a chance to truly to lead the world in the 21st century.
7. The children.

ATTITUDE OF STUDENT-TEACHERS TOWARDS TEACHING PROFESSION

Teaching being a dynamic activity requires a favourable attitude and certain specific competencies from its practitioners. Teachers' proficiency depends on the attitude she possesses for the profession. The positive attitude helps teacher to develop a conductive learner friendly environment in the classroom. This also casts a fruitful effect on learning of the students. Attitude being a social construct is influenced by many factors like gender, social strata, age, and stream of education and previous experience of the job.

The teacher's roles and responsibilities have found extension outside the classroom. The implementation of educational policies, transaction of curricula and spreading awareness are the main areas which keep teacher in the forefront. Changing times have added new dimension to this profession, which requires specified competencies and right attitude. Behaviour, attitude and interest of teacher help in shaping the personality of the student. Attitude is a tendency to react in a particular manner towards the stimuli.

It is a dynamic entity which is subject to change. It is a deciding factor of the teacher's performance. Attitude is defined as a state of readiness shaped through the experience and influences the response of individual towards the stimuli. It is precursor of the behaviour and varies from favourable to unfavourable through neutral. Attitude is made up of three components affective, behavioural and cognitive hence acts as a yardstick of the individual behaviour.

FACTORS AFFECTING THE ATTITUDE OF TEACHERS

Factors which bear influence on the attitude of the teachers are the domestic environment, family background, socio-economic background, beliefs and educational institutes, etc.

School status, school infrastructure, safety conditions in the school, social and professional status all these factors are vital in casting impression on the teachers attitude.

Another factor which casts influence on the attitude is the experience. This holds true for teaching profession also. Teaching experience of the teacher contributes significantly in forming attitude. The teacher's attitude towards the subject and student is significant in creating desire to learn in the students.

Inadequate financial remuneration and delay in payment of salaries are the causes of teacher's having low attitude towards teaching profession. These negative factors when minimized can encourage teachers to be more conscious and responsible towards their duties. Initial teacher training helps in shaping the attitude of student teachers towards teaching profession.

DEVELOPMENT OF POSITIVE ATTITUDE

Development of positive attitude towards profession helps in developing creative thinking and motivating students. The different learning environment, instructional materials and strategies adopted in initial teacher training programme are also responsible for difference in attitude of student teachers towards teaching profession. The type of attitude possessed by the teacher influence the quality of the work accomplished and teaching. Attitude of the teacher has the imprint of competencies that she possesses.

QUALITIES OF PROFESSIONAL TEACHERS

"Teachers are our nation builders—the strength of every profession in our country grows out of the knowledge and skills that teachers help to instil in our children".

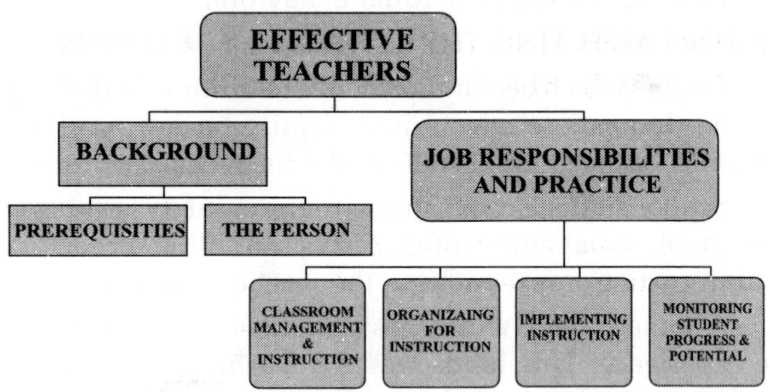

A great teacher is one a student remembers and cherishes forever. Teachers have long-lasting impacts on the lives of their students, and the greatest teachers inspire students toward greatness. To be successful, a great teacher must have:

1. **An Engaging Personality and Teaching Style.** A great teacher is very engaging and holds the attention of students in all discussions.
2. **Clear Objectives for Lessons.** A great teacher establishes clear objectives for each lesson and works to meet those specific objectives during each class.
3. **Effective Discipline Skills.** A great teacher has effective discipline skills and can promote positive behaviours and change in the classroom.
4. **Good Classroom Management Skills.** A great teacher has good classroom management skills and can ensure good student behaviour, effective study and work habits, and an overall sense of respect in the classroom.
5. **Good Communication with Parents.** A great teacher maintains open communication with parents and keeps them informed of what is going on in the classroom as

far as curriculum, discipline, and other issues. They make themselves available for phone calls, meetings, and email.

6. **High Expectations.** A great teacher has high expectations of their students and encourages everyone to always work at their best level.
7. **Knowledge of Curriculum and Standards.** A great teacher has thorough knowledge of the school's curriculum and other standards they must uphold in the classroom. They ensure their teaching meets those standards.
8. **Knowledge of Subject Matter.** This may seem obvious, but is sometimes overlooked. A great teacher has incredible knowledge of and enthusiasm for the subject matter they are teaching. They are prepared to answer questions and keep the material interesting for the students.
9. **Passion for Children and Teaching.** A great teacher is passionate about teaching and working with children. They are excited about influencing students' lives and understand the impact they have.
10. **Strong Rapport with Students.** A great teacher develops a strong rapport with students and establishes trusting relationships.
11. **Friendliness and Congeniality.** I think the most important characteristic of a good teacher can have is to be friendly and congenial with his students. It is a plus if his students can share their problems with him, without being afraid or hesitant. I think students have always thoughts of their teachers as their enemies. With this mentality, they can never be close to each other, and besides that how many teachers did you like who were NOT friendly, and were rather arrogant and rude?
12. **A Good Listener.** Apart from being a good communicator, a good teacher should also have the characteristic of being an even better listener. As there is *Turkish* proverb:

    "If speaking is silver; then listening is gold."

Remember, a good listener will always have many friends and fans. Because people do not want to hear every time, they need people who can listen to them as well. And when a good teacher develops this patient quality in him-self, he starts to become a great teacher.

13. **A Good Sense of Humor.** A good teacher should also have the quality and characteristic of having a good sense of humor. It is a logical fact that a person generally teaches the next generation and as they are younger than the professor, they are expected to have more fun in the class too. So, a good teacher is the one who can keep up with his sense of humor, and with his strong communication skills and personality, can also maintain the discipline of the class.

14. **Kindness.** The last but obviously one of the most important characteristics to have in his box of qualities: he should be a gentle, kind, chivalrous, and benevolent person. Students should love him, and when they do love him, they idolize him. Then ultimately, they will respect him, will do the homework, and eventually will bring greater outputs and results.

TOP FIVE QUALITIES OF EFFECTIVE TEACHERS, ACCORDING TO STUDENTS

Students are most affected by the quality of their teachers. Not only do they interact with teachers every day in the classroom, but the quality of that interaction matters for our students' future. The top five qualities of a great teacher, according to students, are:

1. The ability to develop relationships with their students

The most frequent response is that a great teacher develops relationships with students. The research literature agrees with them: Teachers need to be able to build trusting relationships with students in order to create a safe, positive, and productive learning environment. For example, a student in Boston told us that great teachers are "Willing to listen to students when there is a problem."

2. Patient, caring, and kind personality

Personality characteristics related to being a compassionate person and having sensitivity to student differences, particularly with learners, was the second most frequently reported quality. Again, there is research to support that teacher dispositions are strongly related to student learning and development.

3. Knowledge of learners

This is a broad category that incorporates knowledge of the cognitive, social and emotional development of learners. It includes an understanding of how students learn at a given developmental level; how learning in a specific subject area typically progresses like learning progressions or trajectories; awareness that learners have individual needs and abilities; and an understanding that instruction should be tailored to meet each learner's needs. One student eloquently described it as: "The teacher understands the pace and capacity of the student."

4. Dedication to teaching

Dedication refers to a love of teaching or passion for the work, which includes commitment to students' success. Responses often referred to loving the subject matter or simply being dedicated to the work. To a student, this means a teacher should be "always willing to help and give time."

5. Engaging students in learning

Students also said that teachers should be able to engage and motivate students to learn. Researchers talk about three types of engagement that are required for students to learn: cognitive, emotional, and behavioral. Survey respondents mostly focused on making content interesting and the ability to motivate students to learn. A student in Pennsylvania said great teachers are, "motivating students to succeed in and out of school."

FACULTY DEVELOPMENT PROGRAMS

Today the profession of management teaching has become quite challenging. Business schools teachers are expected to be both effective teachers and researchers. A teacher can "teach" all day long and cover an extensive amount of material, but if students haven't learnt the material, the exercise is an enormous waste of time and energy. Being an educator is not just about sharing knowledge; it is about making sure that learners truly integrate this knowledge and derive learning out of it. Any teaching that does not result in effective learning is useless. Therefore, to be an effective teacher, one needs to be able to deliver the domain knowledge using the most suitable pedagogical tools. An effective teacher is also required to remain at the frontiers of knowledge in his/her areas of subject expertise and gain working knowledge of other domains as management is essentially inter-disciplinary. For this, every teacher needs to continuously upgrade himself/herself by engaging in research.

This Faculty Development Programme (FDP) is aimed at honing the teaching and research skills of prospective, new and seasoned management teachers, researchers and trainers.

The purpose of this program is to provide faculty members an opportunity to strengthen their knowledge of an academic specialty, to broaden or achieve greater depth in a defined field of study, or to achieve competence in a new area of scholarly endeavour.

DEFINITION/DESCRIPTION

Faculty development is a process by which medical school faculty, including preceptors teaching in the clinical setting, work systematically to improve their skills in the following areas:

1. Educational skills
2. Leadership skills
3. Skills necessary to engage in scholarly activities
4. Personal development, and
5. Skills in designing and implementing a professional development plan.

Faculty development activities are successful when individuals' goals in these five areas are being met and when simultaneously the goals of the organization are being met.

Domains/Areas of Faculty Development

- Teaching
- Instructional Design and Curriculum Development
- Scholarly Activity including writing, conducting research, presenting at conferences, etc.
- Leadership, Administration, and Organizational Development
- Personal and Professional Development

Principles

- Strong administrative support
- Reward structures for participation in faculty development programs
- Teaching viewed as a scholarly activity
- Systematic skills development
- Based on principles of adult learning
- Sensitive to identified needs
- Participants learn from each other
- Atmosphere of caring and trust
- Based on collaboration, teamwork, and shared vision
- Celebration of successes.

The Features of Faculty Development that make it Effective

- **The role of experiential learning:** Several authors highlighted that faculty members needed to apply what had been learned during the program, practice skills, and receive feedback on the learned skills.
- **The value of feedback:** Several studies specifically examined the utilization of feedback as a strategy and found that systematic and constructive feedback resulted in improved teaching performance.
- **The importance of peers:** A number of reports stressed on the value of peers as role models, exchanging information and ideas, and the significance of collegial support to promote and maintain change.

- **Adherence to principles of teaching and learning:** Many authors cited principles of adult and experiential learning as an organizing structure for FDPs.
- The use of multiple instructional methods to achieve the learning objectives.

TYPES OF FACULTY DEVELOPMENT PROGRAMME

1. Symposium

Definition

"The symposium forum serves an excellent device for informing an audience, crystallizing opinion and in general preparing the listeners for arriving at decision policies, values, judgment or understanding."

"Symposium consists of a set of program of prepared speeches followed by audience discussion."

"Symposium is a technique in which two or more person under the direction of a chairman present several speeches, which give several aspect of one question."

Objectives:

- To identify and understand two various aspects of the theme.
- To develop the ability to decision and judgment regard a problem.
- To develop the values and feeling regarding a problem.
- To enable the listeners to form policies regarding a theme or problem.

Characteristics:

- It provides the broad understandings of a topic or a problem.
- The opportunity is provided to the listeners to take decision about the problem.
- It is used for higher classes to specific theme and problem.
- It develops the feeling of co-operation and adjustment. The objectives as synthesis and evaluation are achieved by employing the symposium.

- It provides the different views on the topic of the symposium.

Scope for the use of Symposium:

- Use of television for education.
- Scope for the distance education in our education.
- Use of essay and objective type of test.
- Semester system in education.
- Cause of student unrest.
- Quality control of education research.
- Use of microteaching in teacher education.
- Use of team teaching in school.
- Use of action research in classroom teaching.
- Scope of education technology in our education.

Limitation

- The chairman has no control over the speakers.
- There is a probability of repetition of the conduct.
- The different aspect of theme is presented simultaneously.
- The listeners remain passive in the symposium.
- The discussion and presentation of the theme is not summarized at the end.
- This technique is employed to achieve the higher objectives of cognitive domain but affective are not emphasized properly.

Advantages:

- It is suited to a large group or classes.
- This method can be frequently used to present broad topics for discussion at conventions and organization meetings.
- Organization is good because of the set speeches prepared beforehand.
- Gives deeper insight into the topic.
- Directs the students continuously in dependent study.

Disadvantages:

- Inadequate opportunity for all the students to participate actively.
- The speeches are limited to 15-20 minutes.
- Limited audience participation.
- Question and answer limited to 3 or 4 minutes.
- Possibility of overlapping the subjects.

2. Seminar

- Seminar is an instructional technique of higher learning which involves paper reading on a theme and followed by the group discussion to clarify the complex aspects of the theme.
- Illustration.
- Time given.

OBJECTIVES

Cognitive Objectives:

- To develop the higher cognitive abilities: analysis, synthesis and evaluation.
- To develop the ability of keen observation experiences, feelings and to present them effectively.
- To develop the ability to seek clarification and defend the ideas of others effectively.

Affective Objectives:

- To develop the feeling of tolerance on the opposite ideas of others.
- To develop the emotional stability among the participants of the seminar.
- To acquire the good manners of putting questions and answering the questions of others effectively.
- To develop the feelings of co-operation with other colleagues.

Roles of Seminar: In organising a seminar the following roles are performed:

- Organizer or Instructor
- President or Chairman or Convener of the seminar
- Speakers of the day
- Participants and
- Observers.

Types of Seminar:

On the basis of levels and organization the seminars are of four types:

- Mini Seminar
- Main Seminar
- National Seminar
- International Seminar

Advantages:

- The major advantage of seminar as a mode of instruction is testing individual's power of comprehension and evaluation.
- Understanding power and questioning ability in a relevant situation are strengthened.
- Self-reliance, self-confidence, sense of co-operation and responsibility are developed.

Limitation:

- The technique cannot be used for all levels of education. It can be used for higher level of education.
- The person who speaks too much dominates the discussion of the seminar.

3. Workshop

- The word workshop has been borrowed from engineering.
- In workshops, persons have to do some task with their hands to produce something.
- A brief intensive course of education for a small group emphasizing interaction and practical problem solving.

OBJECTIVES

Cognitive Objectives:

- To solve the problems of teaching profession
- To identify the educational objectives in the present context
- To develop an understanding regarding a theme or problem.

Psychomotor Objectives:

To develop the skills to perform a work independently

Advantages:

- It is use to realise the higher cognitive and psychomotor objectives
- It is used for developing and improving professional efficiency
- It develop the feeling of co-operation and group work or team work
- The new practices and innovations of education are introduced by workshop.

Limitations:

- The workshop cannot be organised for the large group so that large number of person are trained
- Generally follow up programmes are not organised in workshop
- The persons do not take interest in practical work or to do something in productive form.

4. Conference

- It is a meeting of large group, organized to discuss current problems and its specifics to provide a workable solution.
- The conference technique has acquired important place in different areas to discuss and solve the problem: Social, Political, Health, Religious and Educational.
- In the area of higher teaching-learning, the conference is one of the most important techniques. The higher

cognitive and effective objectives of education are achieved by employing the conference technique.

OBJECTIVES:

Cognitive objectives:

- To develop analysis, synthesis and evaluation or creative abilities of the participants
- To develop reasoning and critical abilities
- To develop the abilities to study in depth of facts, concepts and problems.

Affective Objectives:

- To develop the tendency to study a fact or concept in broader perspective
- To develop the tendency to emotional balance
- To respect and tolerate anti-ideas and criticism by others
- To develop the feelings of co-operation and freedom of thoughts.

By participating the conference, behavioural skills and good cultural manners start developed among the participants. They are trained to present and defend ideas. They learn how to put questions and how to answer the questions and how the clarification is sought.

Advantages:

- Democratic values are developed among the participants
- It develops the habit of independent study and to think independently on a theme
- Ability of problem-solving is developed among the participants
- Capacity of tolerance of anti-ideas of others is also developed
- Ability of expressing ideas and feelings is developed by attending a conference
- Good manners for asking questions, seeking clarification, presenting own point of view and defending others ideas are developed.

Limitations:

- It is hard to predict attendance. Advance arrangements must be made for conference facilities and housing accommodation.
- Generally the nature of topic is broad; hence discussion is confined to specific issues.
- Group discussion is generally dominated by the good speakers or those who talk too much and do not give opportunities to take part in the discussions.

5. Refresher course

A refresher course is a training course in which people improve their knowledge or skills and learn about new developments that are related to the job that they do.

Refresher Training: Why and When?

There is no saturation point in education – Thomas J. Watson

Why?

It is quite obvious that skills fade with time. There may be various reasons for this degradation of skills. Most often it is because of lack of regular usage of skills and choosing of alternative methods by the employees. Whatsoever the reasons may be, the needs for refresher training have to be identified and addressed, to ensure that the skills are updated and remain current.

Why refresher training is important?

- To retain the existing talent
- To keep pace with the new technologies
- To become the beneficiaries of the current innovations
- To get the best out of your people
- To update with the latest trends
- To bridge the gap between a millennial and a boomer.

When?

Periodic refreshments in training would be a good idea, but most often refresher training can be called for even before the specified period, when the need arises. Generally, it is delivered in cycles once in every 3 or 6 months. Usually this period is decided based upon the kind of job, the skills and the critical safety factors required to do the job. But how can you identify when your existing employees are in need of refresher training?

Here are some signs that help you get to know the need to deliver refresher training to your employees.

- Repeatedly failing to complete the assigned tasks on/in time
- Poor response to training given
- Less output
- Unwilling and indifferent attitudes
- Frequent accidents and safety factors
- Finding it difficult to take-up/accept new concepts

Thus, refresher training boosts up the self-confidence and morale of the employees. It is well-worth it to devote sufficient time to refresh your employees.

Benefits of Faculty Development Program

- Enabling innovation in teaching methods
- Fostering the learning of new skills and knowledge
- Upgrading the skill set of the teacher in order to include technological advancements
- Allowing the opportunity for a teacher to interact with others to find out what is happening in the educational field
- Making a teacher aware of and sensitive to cultural mores and sensibilities
- There are plenty of ways in which such development can be rendered. Some essential aspects go into making up a pretty comprehensive list of ideas for faculty development.

TEACHING AND LEARNING FOR A SUSTAINABLE FUTURE

Education is the most effective means that society possesses for confronting the challenges of the future. Indeed, education will shape the world of tomorrow. Progress increasingly depends upon the products of educated minds: upon research, invention, innovation and adaptation. Of course, educated minds and instincts are needed not only in laboratories and research institutes, but in every walk of life. Education, to be certain, is not the whole answer to every problem. But education, in its broadest sense, must be a vital part of all efforts to imagine and create new relations among people and to foster greater respect for the needs of the environment.

- Education today does not sufficiently prepare learners to contribute to sustainable development.
- Themes like climate change or biodiversity need to be integrated into teaching and learning.
- Teaching and learning needs to be designed in a participatory, learner-centred way.

What is education for Sustainable Development?

Education for Sustainable Development (ESD) processes emphasize the need for stimulating a holistic, integrated and interdisciplinary approach to developing the knowledge and skills needed for a sustainable future as well as changes in values, behaviour and lifestyles.

Education for a sustainable development places education at the heart of the quest to build a fairer, less troubled and more peaceful world. This makes education not just an end in itself – as important as the intrinsic goals of education are -but also one of the most powerful instruments for bringing about the changes required to achieve sustainable development. Teachers, of course, are vital actors in this process and teacher education a key mechanism for building capacity for a sustainable future.

Aims:

- Promote understanding of the interdependence of natural, socio-economic and political systems at local, national and global levels.
- Encourage critical reflection and decision making that is reflected in personal lifestyles

- Engage the active participation of the citizenry in building sustainable development.

Objectives:

- To develop an appreciation of the scope and purpose of educating for a sustainable future.
- To clarify concepts and themes related to sustainable development and how they can be integrated in all subject areas across the school curriculum.
- To enhance skills for integrating issues of sustainability into a range of school subjects and classroom topics.
- To enhance skills for using a wide range of interactive and learner-centred teaching and learning strategies that underpin the knowledge, critical thinking, values and citizenship objectives implicit in reorienting education towards sustainable development.
- To encourage wider awareness of Information and Communication Technologies (ICTs), the potential of multimedia-based approaches to education and the potential of the Internet as a rich source of educational materials.
- To enhance skills in computer literacy and multimedia education.

Principles:

- Care for each other and value social justice and peace
- Protect natural systems and use resources wisely
- Value appropriate development and satisfying livelihoods for all
- Make decisions through fair and democratic means.

Characteristics of Sustainable Development:

- Need of society
- Expectation of qualitative development
- Thinking of present as well as future
- Social, biotic and economic factors are considered
- Balance between profit and loss.

OVERVIEW

Teaching and Learning for a Sustainable Future is a multimedia teacher education program published by UNESCO. It contains 100 hours (divided into 27 modules) of professional development for use in pre-service teacher courses as well as the in-service education of teachers, curriculum developers, education policy makers, and authors of educational materials.

UNESCO and the international community in general, believe that we need to foster – through education – the values, behavior, and lifestyles required for a sustainable future. Teaching and Learning for a Sustainable Future is rooted in a new vision of education that helps students better understand the world in which they live, addressing the complexity and interconnectedness of problems such as poverty, wasteful consumption, environmental degradation, population, health, conflict and human rights that threaten our future.

Teaching and Learning for a Sustainable Future will enable teachers to plan learning experiences that empower their students to develop and evaluate alternative visions of a sustainable future and to work creatively with others to help bring their visions of a better world into effect. It will also enhance the computer literacy of teachers and build their skills in using multimedia-based resources and strategies in their teaching.

UNESCO, EDUCATION FOR A SUSTAINABLE FUTURE

Teaching and Learning for a Sustainable Future is one of several programs initiated by UNESCO's program on educating for a Sustainable Future. It has been developed by UNESCO in its function as task manager for the International Work Program on Education, Public Awareness and Training for Sustainability of the United Nations Commission on Sustainable Development and for the 2002 World Summit on Sustainable Development.

TOWARDS A SUSTAINABLE FUTURE

Thinking about the Future - No one knows what the future will be, except that it will be very different from what life is today and that decisions about whether the future is a sustainable one or not will depend upon changes in human culture.

Our culture includes our whole system of beliefs, values, attitudes, customs and institutions. It shapes our gender, race and other social relations, and affects the way we perceive ourselves and the world and how we interact with other people and the rest of nature. To the extent that the global crisis facing humanity is a reflection of collective values and lifestyles, it is, above all, a cultural crisis. Culture, therefore, has a central place in the complex notion of sustainability – and whatever form the future takes, it will be shaped at the local level by the mosaic of cultures that surround the globe and which contribute to the decisions that each country, community, household and individual makes.

Our increasing awareness of many pressing global realities is helping us to understand the impact of human actions on the environment and on human quality of life. Indeed, the concept of sustainability is, in itself, a reflection of this growing awareness and of the need for new cultural values. Thus, it has been suggested that:

Perhaps we are beginning to move towards a new global ethic which transcends all other systems of allegiance and belief, which is rooted in a consciousness of the interrelatedness and sanctity of life. Would such a common ethic have the power to motivate us to modify our current dangerous course? There is obviously no ready answer to this question, except to say that without a moral and ethical foundation, sustainability is unlikely to become a reality.

Local and national communities are applying this ethic in many different ways and developing images of sustainable futures that are both culturally appropriate and locally relevant. The great diversity of cultures around the world means that there will be many versions of what a 'sustainable future' might be like and many different local forms of sustainability. Despite these differences, there are at least three common themes in global thinking about sustainable futures. These include the ideas that sustainability involves: thinking about forever; a process of learning; and, a dynamic balance.

THINKING ABOUT FOREVER

Underlying all our images of a sustainable future is the key principle that sustainability is about 'thinking about forever'.

This means committing ourselves to the common good by thinking differently, considering things previously forgotten, broadening our perspectives, clarifying what we value, connecting with our neighbors, and providing hope for future generations.

Building the capacity to think in terms of 'forever' is a key task of education.

A PROCESS OF LEARNING

Educating for a sustainable future is not so much about a destination as about the process of learning to make decisions that consider the long-term economy, ecology and equity of all communities. Its goal is to build an enduring society. This involves learning how to anticipate the consequences of our actions envision a sustainable future and create the steps needed to achieve the vision. Individuals and societies will perpetually have to make choices. How those choices are made and the information and ethical discernment used in making them will determine whether our visions of a sustainable future are achieved.

The World Commission on Environment and Development urged people, governments and businesses around the world to make their choices that contributed to ways of living and relating to the Earth and each other so that the use of resources today would meet 'the needs of the present without compromising the ability of future generations to meet their own needs.'

How can the needs of current and future generations be met in a world where the aspirations of many people far exceed their needs and the life chances of the many more are acutely limited by poverty and environmental decline? The task of creating social, economic and political systems that meet our needs and aspirations, that are based on sound ecological principles, and that are democratic and fair to current and future generations, is a deeply challenging one. Yet, building the capacity and commitment to build such a sustainable future is, in large part, one of the tasks of education. This requires that teachers and schools have a vision of what a sustainable future might be like – bearing in mind the dynamic balance between cultural differences and the emerging global ethic of 'interrelatedness and sanctity of life'.

A DYNAMIC BALANCE

The dynamic balance between cultural differences and this emerging global ethic is a key concept in educating for a sustainable future. It reminds us that sustainability will be built from the actions of people and businesses in their own communities, at local levels, and extend outwards in a spiral of shared understandings and revised and renewed visions.

Teaching and Learning for a Sustainable Future does not prescribe the forms that a sustainable future might take. Rather, it encourages adaptations and applications of the learning activities to local situations and needs. Nevertheless, in keeping with the emerging global ethic of 'interrelatedness and sanctity of life', the learning activities reflect a dynamic balance among four dimensions and principles that underlie a sustainable future.

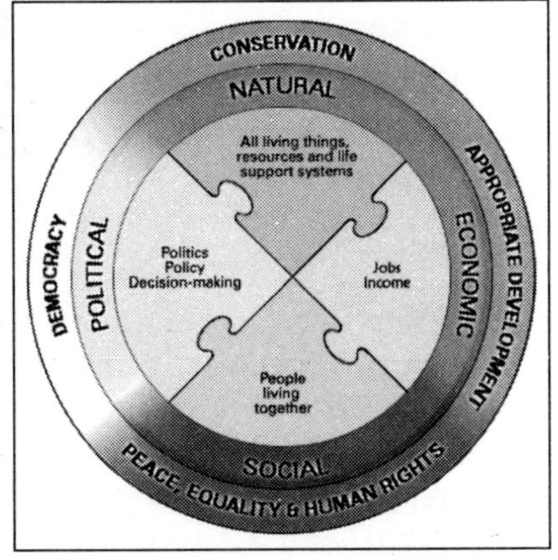

Dimension of Sustainability		Value Principle
Social Sustainability	↔	Peace and Equity
Ecological Sustainability	↔	Conservation
Economic Sustainability	↔	Appropriate Development
Political Sustainability	↔	Democracy

CONCLUSION

In this unit, we explored the aspect of teaching as a profession, different methods of teaching, various roles played by the teacher in changing learning environment. Teacher imparts knowledge or skill through while facilitators create an environment where students acquire knowledge by doing activities by themselves. By being a reflective practitioner, the teacher should be able to develop their professional development activities which emphasise the teachers as a learner and also as a professional. The recent changing role of teacher has been identified as co-learner rather than a facilitator as new technologies have been making tremendous changes in the instructional strategy of teaching.

QUESTIONS

1. What are the characteristics of effective and ineffective teaching?
2. Write short notes on the nature of teaching.
3. Critically examine the importance of Teaching as a profession.
4. Enumerate the qualities of professional teacher.
5. Write an essay on teaching and learning for sustainable future.

References

Aggarwal, J.C. (1996). *Teachers and Education in a Developing Society*. New Delhi: Vikas Publishing Pvt. Ltd.

Astin, Alexander W., Helen S. Astin, and Jennifer A. Lindholm. 2010. *Cultivating the Spirit: How College Can Enhance Students' Inner Lives*. San Francisco: Jossey-Bass.

Ausubel, David (1963) The Psychology of meaningful Verbal Learning, New York: Grune and Books Private Limited.

Bracey, G.W. "Why Can't They be Like We Were?" *Phi Delta Kappan* 73 (October 1991): 104-117.

Bruner, J., Goodnow, J.J. and Austin, G.A. (1956): A Study of Thinking. New York: John Wiley.

Catherine Twomey Fosnet (2003) Constructivism - Theory, Perspectives and Practice, Teachers College Press, Sage Publications, Delhi.

DeWitt, J. and Storksdieck, M. (2008) A Short Review of School Field Trips: Key Findings from the Past and Implications for the Future, *Visitor Studies*, 11(2), pp. 181-197.

Hawley, R.C. (1982). *Ten Steps for Motivating Reluctant Learners*. Amherst, MA: Education Research Associates.

Kochhar, S.K (1985) Methods and Techniques of Teaching. New Delhi: Sterling Publishers'.

Laws, K. (1989) Learning Geography through Fieldwork, in Fien, J., Gerber, R. and Wilson, P. (eds) *The Geography Teacher's Guide to the Classroom*, 2nd Edition, Macmillan, Melbourne.

Liversidge, T., Cochrane, M., Kerfoot, B. & Thomas, J. (2009). Teaching Science, New Delhi. Lokman Ali, (2012). *Teacher Education*, APH Publishing Corporation, New Delhi.

Marchese, T.J. (1997). The New Conversations about Learning: Insights from Neuroscience and Anthropology, Cognitive Science and Work-place Studies." In Assessing Impact: Evidence and Action, pp. 79-95. Washington, DC: American Association for Higher Education.

Mayer, R. E. (2004). Should there be a Three-strike Rule against Pure Discovery Learning? American Psychologist, 59(1), 14-19.

McKinney, Kathleen. (2010). Active Learning. Normal, IL. Center for Teaching, Learning & Technology. Private Limited. Stratteninc. Teachers of Secondary Stage. New Delhi: NCERT.

Morganett, L.L. "Good Teacher-Student Relationships: A Key Element in Classroom Motivation and Management." *Education* 112 (Winter 1991): 260-264.

Pianta, R.C., Hamre, B., & Stuhlman, M. (2003). *Relationships between Teachers and Children*. Handbook of Psychology.

Quintana, C., Shin, N., Norris, C., & Soloway, E. (2006). Learner-centered design: Reflections on the past and directions for the future. In R. K. Sawyer (ed.), The Cambridge handbook of the learning sciences (pp. 119-134), Cambridge, MA: Cambridge University Press.

Rogers, A. (ed) (1995) *Taking Action: An Environmental Guide For You and Your Community*, United Nations Environment Programme, Nairobi.

Sharma, S. (2006). Constructivist Approaches to Teaching and Learning Hand Book.

Smith, M. (2002) Exploring a Changing World: A Guide to Fieldwork for Youth Expeditions, Young Explorers Trust.

Spaulding, C.L. *Motivation in the Classroom*. New York: McGraw-Hill, 1992.

Thangasamy, Kohila. (2016) Teach Gently, Chennai: Pavai Pathipagam.

The Cambridge handbook of the learning sciences.

Thorndike, E.L.(1905), The Elements of Psychology. New York: A.G. Seiler.

Vijoyprakash,(2007) Creative Learning a Handbook for Teachers and Trainers. New Delhi: Viva.

Wentzel, K.R. (2012). *Teacher-Student Relationships and Adolescent Competence at School*. In Interpersonal Relationships in Education (pp. 19-35). Sense Publishers.

Wlodkowski, R.J. (1986). *Motivation and Teaching: A Practical Guide*. Washington, DC: National Education Association.

Yogesh Kumar Singh & Ruchika Nath, (2013). *Teacher Education*, New Delhi: APH Publishing Corporation.

archive.mu.ac.in/mywebtest/

https://www.ijhsss.com/

ww-infed.org/schooling/inf – sch.htm

www.bigpicture.org.au/learning-cycle-reference-book

http://ctl.byu.edu/tip/active-learning-techniques

https://en.m.wikipedia.org/wiki/constructivism

https://exploratorium.ed

u/education www.merriam.webster.com www.indiastudy channel.com

http://www.explorelearning.com

http://www.oblockbooks.com

oblockbooks@worldnet.att.net.

http://EzineArticles.com

Study Material from TNTEU.

Index

F

G

I

K

L